RICE UNIVERSITY STUDIES

MONOGRAPH IN MUSIC

ESSAYS ON THE MONTEVERDI MASS AND VESPERS OF 1610

JEFFREY G. KURTZMAN

PUBLISHED BY
WILLIAM MARSH RICE UNIVERSITY
HOUSTON, TEXAS

Vol. 64, No. 4   Fall 1978

784.1
m78zk

Library of Congress Catalog No. 78-66039

US-ISSN-0035-4996

US-ISBN-0-89263-238-0

RICE UNIVERSITY STUDIES

Vol. 64, No. 4   Fall 1978

ESSAYS ON THE MONTEVERDI MASS AND VESPERS OF 1610

INTRODUCTION

The essays in this volume were originally conceived separately with a view toward publication in various musicological journals. However, the opportunity to bring together in one issue of RICE UNIVERSITY STUDIES a series of essays focusing on the single subject of Monteverdi's Mass and Vespers print of 1610 has obvious advantages for both the author and his readers.

Chapter V, "Some Historical Perspectives on the Monteverdi Vespers," has previously appeared in *Analecta Musicologica* **15** (1975): 29-86, and is reprinted here, revised and updated, with the kind permission of the editor of *Analecta*, Dr. Friedrich Lippmann. Chapters III, IV, and V are based upon my Ph.D. dissertation, "The Monteverdi Vespers of 1610 and their Relationship with Italian Sacred Music of the Early Seventeenth Century" (University of Illinois at Urbana-Champaign, 1972). These three essays consolidate and summarize the analyses and conclusions of several chapters from that dissertation.

Chapters I and II are the result of additional research undertaken in preparation for my forthcoming critical edition of the *Missa In illo tempore* and *Vespro della Beata Vergine,* to be published by the Fondazione "Claudio Monteverdi" of Cremona, Italy, in its series, *Claudio Monteverdi: Opera Omnia.*

Each of the five chapters approaches a specific issue raised by the Mass and Vespers. Chapter I examines the two sources of these works, one a manuscript copy in the *Biblioteca Apostolica Vaticana* preserving only the Mass, and the other Ricciardo Amadino's print of 1610 containing both the Mass and Vespers. An investigation of the original sources is collated with other seventeenth-century source materials and studies in an attempt to answer questions of notation and performance practice. The discussion of *chiavette* and transposition in this chapter leads to conclusions about tonal relationships somewhat different from those originally proposed in my dissertation.

Chapter II is a critical essay on the *Missa In illo tempore.* The object of this inquiry is not a detailed analysis of the Mass, but a general assessment

1

of the work's main characteristics, artistic merits, and significance in Monteverdi's compositional career.

Chapters III and IV are more thoroughly analytical, attempting to demonstrate in detail some of the most important compositional procedures in the Vespers. Attention is centered on parody and variation techniques throughout the Vespers and a sample case of melodic construction in the motet *Nigra sum*.

In chapter V, the Vespers are evaluated in relation to their background. A historical perspective is developed through a review of late sixteenth- and early seventeenth-century Italian Vesper repertoire and a comparison between Vesper and motet music of the early seventeenth century and Monteverdi's own styles and techniques. Conclusions are also drawn as to the impact of Monteverdi's *Vespro* on other Italian composers in the decade 1610-1620.

Until recently, when one spoke of the Monteverdi Vespers, it was not even clear what was meant or what compositions constituted these Vespers in the first place. The succession of pieces after the Mass in Amadino's print is as follows:

> *Domine ad adiuvandum* (respond)
> *Dixit Dominus* (psalm 109)
> *Nigra sum* (motet)
> *Laudate pueri* (psalm 112)
> *Pulchra es* (motet)
> *Laetatus sum* (psalm 121)
> *Duo Seraphim* (motet)
> *Nisi Dominus* (psalm 126)
> *Audi coelum* (motet)
> *Lauda Jerusalem* (psalm 147)
> *Sonata sopra "Sancta Maria ora pro nobis"* (instrumental sonata
>   with litany)
> *Ave maris stella* (hymn)
> *Magnificat* for seven voices and six instruments
> *Magnificat* for six voices.

Monteverdi's publication has been termed by Hans Redlich "a loose collection of diverse liturgical compositions rather than . . . a single artistic unit."[1] Leo Schrade, in his biography of Monteverdi, recognized that the respond, psalms, hymn, and *Magnificat*s were the standard liturgical items for Vespers on feasts of the Virgin.[2] Schrade also drew associations between the texts of two of the motets and antiphons for Marian Vespers.[3] But others were still troubled by the fact that none of these motet texts is strictly in agreement with any liturgical antiphon for Vespers of the Virgin. These writers have therefore claimed that the motets were distinctly separate from the official liturgical items in Monteverdi's print.[4]

In the last ten years, however, it has been demonstrated by several scholars that sacred services in the seventeenth century were not limited exclusively to published liturgical texts, despite the frequent attempts of Rome to eliminate elements not officially sanctioned.[5] Evidence of the performance of sacred compositions whose texts fall outside the official liturgy has accumulated to the point where there is now a general consensus that Monteverdi's *Vespro* can appropriately be performed as a complete artistic unit, consistent with seventeenth-century religious practices.[6]

Recognition of the artistic and liturgical integrity of the Vespers does not mean that a complete performance is the only way the music may have been presented in Monteverdi's time or should be heard today. Flexibility was characteristic not only of early seventeenth-century musical styles, but also of performance practices and performance conditions. This flexibility is announced by Monteverdi on his title page, which indicates that at least some of the music of the print is suitable for use in chapels or the chambers of princes.[7] Flexibility in the manner of performance is explicitly stated in the music itself where instrumental *ritornelli* are designated optional in *Dixit Dominus* and the instruments are *si placet* in the respond. The *ritornelli* in the hymn, without rubrics, may also be considered optional.

The two *Magnificats* in the collection likewise suggest multiple possibilities for performance, since only one *Magnificat* is required for Vespers. As demonstrated in chapter III, the two settings of the canticle are intimately related to one another; the most prominent difference is that one employs a large number of *obbligato* instruments while the other is furnished with only an organ continuo. It seems evident from these two *Magnificats*, as well as the optional *ritornelli* and the designation of instruments *si placet,* that a grandiose, festal celebration of Vespers complete with the coloration of instruments was only one of the performance possibilities envisioned by Monteverdi. In such a solemn setting the *ritornelli* would be performed, the full respond and *Sonata sopra Sancta Maria* with their large instrumental forces would be included, and the *Magnificat* with *obbligato* instruments would be chosen. But for churches and occasions where instruments were not available or not deemed appropriate, the reduced respond, the psalms, the motets, the hymn, and the alternate *Magnificat* without instruments could still provide a lengthy and elaborate Vesper service.[8]

Still other, more limited possibilities may be considered. There is no reason to believe that the performance of polyphony for one portion of a sacred service necessitated polyphonic performances of all liturgical items.[9] Certainly the motets could have been omitted, especially since they required virtuoso singers not readily available in most churches. A choir master might also have selected only one or several of the psalms without using them all. A service could have been mostly in plainchant with the only polyphony consisting of Monteverdi's hymn or the *Magnificat* without instruments. Pieces selected from the Amadino print could well have been mixed with psalms, motets, or a Magnificat from other Vesper collections. And, as implied by Monteverdi's title page, portions of the print could have served singly or collectively as private devotional music outside the church.

Such a multiplicity of options vastly increased the usefulness of Monteverdi's collection, and this utility must be recognized as an important consideration for composers and publishers of sacred music in the seventeenth century.[10] We must also recognize that an exclusive concern for scholarly precision and accuracy can at times actually distort reality in seeking definitive solutions to issues and practices where flexibility, improvisation, and continual variety were primary objectives. Many a study and edition of the Vespers has been marred by the attempt to be definitive. Style and taste can be documented generally and understood through experience, but they do not yield very successfully to efforts at establishing precise, scientifically demonstrable criteria of evaluation. In such matters informed and experienced judgment is the appropriate goal of scholarship, and it is hoped that the essays presented here will contribute to an informed understanding of the Monteverdi Mass and Vespers on the part of both scholars and practical musicians.

In the course of my studies of the Monteverdi Mass and Vespers, I have accumulated numerous debts to librarians and fellow scholars. I wish to acknowledge, first of all, a special debt to Professor Charles Hamm, who has served over the past fifteen years in many capacities: as teacher, as friend, and as advisor for two separate theses. His wise counsel and trenchant criticism were invaluable in the preparation of my dissertation. My colleague, Professor Anne Schnoebelen, has also given generously of her time and experience in reading and criticizing various chapters. Professors William Harris of Middlebury College and Kristine Wallace of Rice University have been helpful in matters of Latin grammar. Professor Wallace supplied the translation of Monteverdi's dedication in chapter I. The musical examples in chapters I-IV were painstakingly prepared by Robert Walker.

Among librarians, I owe particular thanks to Sergio Paganelli of the Civico Museo Bibliografico Musicale of Bologna, Italy, for numerous kindnesses and a constantly growing friendship. Thanks are also due to many librarians and libraries that have provided me with microfilms and otherwise assisted my research. These include Signora Bonavera and the staff of the Civico Museo Bibliografico of Bologna, William McClellan of the University of Illinois at Urbana-Champaign, Emilio Maggini of the Biblioteca del Seminario in Lucca, Antonio Brasini of the Biblioteca Comunale in Cesena, Siro Cisilino of the Cini Foundation in Venice; the Biblioteca Comunale in Assisi, the Biblioteca Capitolare in Verona, the University Library in Wroclaw, Poland, the University Library in Uppsala, Sweden, and the British Library.

My research in Italian sacred music of the early seventeenth century has brought me into contact with a number of outstanding scholars who have unselfishly shared their ideas and information with me and from whose friendship I have profited in other ways. I wish to acknowledge especially Professors James Armstrong, Denis Arnold, Stephen Bonta, George Nugent, Pierluigi Petrobelli, Jerome Roche, and Howard Smither.

Stephen Bonta, Howard Smither, and Professor Richard Butler of Rice University read the entire manuscript, offering many valuable suggestions and criticisms. I have tried to take as many of their recommendations as possible into consideration in preparation of the final copy, but must assume responsibility myself for the ultimate form of this volume, including its inevitable errors. Whatever advice I have been unable to follow does not lessen my appreciation of their efforts. Special acknowledgment must also go to Kathleen Murfin, Associate Editor of RICE UNIVERSITY STUDIES, whose editorial acumen, uncanny eye, and unfailing cheerfulness and optimism have seen this book smoothly through the press. The way has also been smoothed by a special publication grant from Rice University and from the Shepherd School of Music.

No amount of thanks can express the gratitude I owe my wife, Kathi, for her infinite patience, encouragement, and moral support.

NOTES

1. Hans F. Redlich, "Claudio Monteverdi: Some Problems of Textual Interpretation," *Musical Quarterly* **41**, no. 1 (January 1955): 68.

2. Leo Schrade, *Monteverdi, Creator of Modern Music* (New York: W. W. Norton & Company, Inc., 1950), pp. 251-254.

3. Ibid.

4. See especially Denis Stevens, "Where are the Vespers of Yesteryear?" *Musical Quarterly* **47**, no. 3 (July 1961): 316-325; and Giuseppe Biella, "La 'Messa' il 'Vespro' e i 'Sacri Concenti' di Claudio Monteverdi," *Musica sacra*, serie seconda, **9** (1964): 105-115.

5. The most important articles demonstrating the flexibility of liturgical practice are Stephen Bonta, "Liturgical Problems in Monteverdi's Marian Vespers," *Journal of the American Musicological Society* **20**, no. 1 (Spring 1967): 87-106; Wolfgang Osthoff, "Unità liturgica e artistica nei 'Vespri' del 1610," *Rivista italiana di Musicologia* **2**, no. 2 (1967): 314-327; and James Armstrong, "The 'Antiphonae, seu Sacrae Cantiones' (1613) of Giovanni Francesco Anerio: A Liturgical Study," *Analecta Musicologica* **14** (1974): 89-150. Additional supporting evidence is offered in chapter V, pp. 127-131 of this book.

6. A discussion of artistic unity in the Vespers can be found in my dissertation, "The Monteverdi Vespers of 1610 and their Relationship with Italian Sacred Music of the Early Seventeenth Century" (University of Illinois at Urbana-Champaign, 1972), pp. 69-248. As mentioned above, the conclusions on tonal relationships have been modified in chapter I of this volume.

7. *Sanctissimae Virgini/Missa Senis Vocibus/ac Vesperae Pluribus/Decantandae,/cum Nonnullis Sacris Concentibus,/ad Sacella sive Principum Cubicula accommodata./Opera/a Claudio Monteverde/nuper effecta/ac Beatiss. Paulo V. Pont. Max. Consecrata./Venetijs, Apud Ricciardum Amadinum./MDCX.* The meaning of the phrase *"ad Sacella sive Principum Cubicula accommodata"* and the items to which it applies has been the subject of considerable controversy. See Redlich, "Claudio Monteverdi," Schrade, *Monteverdi,* and Stevens, "Where are the Vespers." The grammar of the title does not adhere to classical practice and is ambiguous as to the items referenced under the phrase *"ad Sacella . . . accommodata."* Attempts to derive definitive conclusions from the title are therefore misdirected.

8. The idea of one service with instruments and one without was first suggested by Biella, "La 'Messa' il 'Vespro,' " p. 114.

9. See Frank A. D'Accone's study of polyphony in sacred services in Florence in "The Musical Chapels at the Florentine Cathedral and Baptistry During the First Half of the 16th Century," *Journal of the American Musicological Society* **24,** no. 1 (Spring 1971): 1-50. See especially the list of feasts and polyphonic items on pp. 4-5.

10. For a fuller discussion of multiple options in Vesper collections of the late sixteenth and early seventeenth centuries, see chapter V, pp. 124-131.

CHAPTER I

THE MASS AND VESPERS OF 1610:
THE SOURCES AND THEIR INTERPRETATION

All musical notation is ambiguous and in need of interpretation, even the most extravagantly detailed notations of the twentieth century. But the musical sources of the early Baroque era pose especially difficult problems for scholars precisely because flexibility and ambiguity in notation and the manner of performance were primary elements of early seventeenth-century style. There can be no absolute determination of "authentic" interpretation in a period whose documents unequivocally testify to a wide range of acceptable performing methods. Seventeenth-century musicians themselves sometimes strayed beyond the bounds of what many composers considered good taste. Admonitions to performers appended to numerous early *Seicento* music prints demonstrate how important appropriate execution was to composers and how often they thought it necessary to describe aspects of performance that could not be taken for granted. Some of these prefaces grew to be treatises of major significance, providing modern scholars with invaluable evidence about contemporary techniques. These sources are themselves often mutually contradictory, however, still leaving room for legitimate disagreement on many issues. The most the modern scholar or musician can hope for is that experience with the documentary and musical evidence as well as with Baroque instruments will eventually lead to judgment and taste compatible with the performance concepts and practices of this problematic period. The term "authentic" can only have meaning for the early Baroque within this framework of uncertainty and ambiguity. Definitive answers are out of the question.

Ricciardo Amadino's print of Monteverdi's Mass and Vespers of 1610 is one of those documents whose close study, coupled with additional evidence from other sources, yields useful information on the range of possibilities envisioned by the composer for his music. At the same time, this print is rife with problems and questions demanding interpretation and resolution. Just as the Mass and Vespers constitute a compendium of nearly every style of sacred music of the early seventeenth century, Amadino's print poses virtually all the problems of interpretation encountered by the modern scholar or performer in attempting to come to grips with the music of that era.

The Introduction to this volume has already outlined the liturgical ambiguities of Monteverdi's collection and the various combinations of pieces that could be presented, depending upon the solemnity of the Marian feast being celebrated, the instruments and singers available, or the surroundings in which the music was to be heard.

This multiplicity of possibilities concerns merely the initial selection of pieces, or even parts of pieces, from the print. But in addition to these options, other purely musical questions and ambiguities arise from the improvisatory character of early Baroque music. Basso continuo realization, organ registration, *ad libitum* accompanying and doubling of vocal parts with instruments, instrumental and vocal ornamentation, and *musica ficta* were all issues to be settled anew each time the music, especially the Vespers in the new style, was to be performed. Monteverdi's notation is actually much more detailed with regard to some of these matters than that of his contemporaries, but he nevertheless left many elements of performance unspecified.

Other problems of interpretation emerge from errors in Amadino's print and from differences between the two sources of the *Missa In illo tempore.* A comparison between the sources of the Mass and a close study of errors in the print are essential for obtaining the best possible reading for a critical edition. F rtunately, it is usually much easier to arrive at decisions in these matters than in questions of performance practice, and the preference of one version over another can often be adequately demonstrated.

The present essay will examine the uncertainties and problems in Amadino's print and the manuscript of the Mass, beginning with the sources and their relationship to one another, proceeding to a study of errors and inconsistencies in the print, and concluding with an examination of the *Bassus Generalis* part-book and performance practice.

THE SOURCES

Amadino's print of 1610, containing both the Mass and Vespers, comprises seven part-books, *Cantus, Altus, Tenor, Bassus, Quintus, Sextus,* and *Septimus,* plus a separate part-book in folio entitled *Bassus Generalis.*[1]

The *Missa In illo tempore* also exists in a second source, *Cappella Sistina* Ms. 107 of the *Biblioteca Apostolica Vaticana,* whose version of the work is not identical to Amadino's. Its title reads: *Sanctiss. Virgini/Missa/Senis Vocibus/A Claudio Monteverde/Nuper Effecta/ac Beatiss. Paulo V. P.O.M./Consecrata.* This manuscript is not a holograph copy, for the inscription continues: *quam/ab Edaci Atramento/Penitus Fere Corrosam/Ioseph Vecchius/Magister Cap. Pont. Nunc Existens/ob Supradicti*

Pontificis/Memoriam/et Tanti Viri Excellentiam/Sedente/Innocentio XI. P.O.M./Restitui Curavit/An. M.DC.LXXXIII. At the bottom of the page in very small script is the name of the copyist: *Bartholomaeus Belleschus scribebat Anno ut supra.* Even this restoration, necessitated by the corrosive effects of the original ink, did not suffice permanently, for the title page is preceded by another folio testifying to a second restoration: *Sedente/ Benedicto XIII/P.O.M./Sub protectione Em̄i, & Rm̄i D. Petri Presbyt./ Card. Otthoboni/Tit. S. Laurentii in Damaso/S.R.E. Vice Cancelarii/R.D. Petro Bastianello de Triviniano/Magistro Capp. Pont. pro tempore existente/Restauravit Anno D./MDCCXXIV.* The manuscript contains the same dedication to Pope Paul V as Amadino's print with only slight differences of orthography. There is no *Bassus Generalis* in the Vatican manuscript since performances in the Sistine Chapel did not use accompanying instruments of any kind.

Yet a third version of the Mass survives in an organ *partitura* compiled by a certain Lorenzo Tonelli and appended to a Brescian copy of the Amadino print lacking only the *Bassus Generalis.*[2] Tonelli's *partitura* includes all of the voices plus the *Bassus Generalis,* proving that the latter part-book was available to him at one time. This manuscript is therefore not a primary source for the work, but it is instructive with regard to performance practice, as will be seen below.

Questions and uncertainties concerning the Mass and Vespers begin with the relationship between the two principal sources of the former. The restored Vatican manuscript carries no original date, not even at the conclusion of the dedication. The dedication in the Amadino print, on the other hand, is dated with precision *Venetijs Calendis Septemb. 1610* (September 1, 1610). What documentary information exists surrounding the presentation of the Mass to Pope Paul V in Rome and the publication of the entire Mass and Vespers in Venice is at some points contradictory. In addition, a misdated letter of Monteverdi's has contributed to further confusion and untenable speculations.[3]

The first mention of the Mass and Vespers is in a letter from the Mantuan singer Bassano Casola to Cardinal Ferdinando Gonzaga in Rome, dated July 16, 1610.[4] In this correspondence Casola describes Monteverdi's recent compositional activity and his intention to visit the Holy City:

Il Monteverdi fa stampare una Messa da Cappella a sei voci di studio et fatica grande, essendosi obligato maneggiar sempre in ogni nota per tutte le vie, sempre più rinforzando le otto fughe che sono nel motetto, *in illo tempore* del *Gomberti* e fà stampare unitamente ancora di Salmi del Vespero della Madonna, con varie et diverse maniere d'inventioni et armonia, et tutte sopra il canto fermo, con pensiero di venirsene a Roma questo Autumno, per dedicarli a Sua Santità. Và ancho preparando una muta di Madrigali a cinque voci, che sarà di tre pianti quello dell'Arianna con il solito canto sempre, il pianto di Leandro et Hereo del Marini, il terzo, datoglielo, da S.A.Sma. di Pastore che sia morta la sua Ninfa. Parole del figlio del Sigr. Conte Lepido Agnelli in morte della Signora Romanina.[5]

Casola's description of the Mass and Vespers is neither complete nor accurate in every detail. The *otto fughe* from the Gombert motet are actually ten in number. In mentioning the *Salmi del Vespero, tutte sopra il canto fermo,* Casola has in mind the five Vesper psalms and very probably the two *Magnificats,* but he omits any reference to the respond, motets, hymn, and *Sonata sopra Sancta Maria,* which are also included in Amadino's print. Whatever inaccuracies and omissions there may be in Casola's remarks, it is nevertheless evident that Monteverdi's work seems to have been largely if not entirely finished by this date, a circumstance that would certainly have been necessary for the publication to be issued on September 1.

Also of some note in Casola's letter is the list of laments in preparation, two of which were published four years later in the Sixth Book of Madrigals.[6] There was often a substantial time lag between the completion of Monteverdi's compositions and their eventual publication. Some of the madrigals from Book IV (1603) and Book V (1605) were already in circulation by 1600, as proven by the discussion and quotation of excerpts in *L'Artusi, ovvero, Delle imperfezioni della moderna musica,* printed in that year.[7] *L'Orfeo* was premiered in the spring of 1607 but not published in its first edition until 1609. Casola's letter shows a four-year delay in the appearance of the laments.

These apparently normal time lags suggest that part or perhaps even all of the Mass and Vespers may have been completed well before the late summer of 1610. The close connections between portions of the Vespers and *L'Orfeo* also imply an early date for some of the pieces, especially the respond *Domine ad adiuvandum,* which is contrafacted from the opera's *Toccata.* It is, in fact, quite possible that the compositions in Amadino's very large print of 1610 represent a gradual accumulation of material over the span of several years. Preparations for the Gonzaga wedding celebration of 1608, about which Monteverdi complained bitterly in a letter long after the festivities were over, occupied all his time in the fall of 1607 and the spring of 1608, leaving him exhausted at the beginning of the summer.[8] But work on the Mass and Vespers may have progressed during the summer of 1607, the summer and fall of 1608, and throughout much of 1609. Some of the pieces in the print, particularly the conservative psalm *Nisi Dominus,* could conceivably date from even earlier than 1607, although there is no substantiating evidence.

Unlike *L'Orfeo* and *Arianna,* the Mass and Vespers do not seem to have been written on command for a special occasion, and there is no record of a Mantuan presentation of any of this music, although performance of at least some pieces is highly likely.[9] Monteverdi may not have been under any pressure in the composition of these works other than his own wish to publish proof of his abilities in multiple styles of sacred music. His desire to escape the Gonzaga court, expressed in his father's letters to the Duke and

Duchess, may have led to the preparation of a collection designed to open opportunities for a church position free from the demands and intrigues of the Gonzaga household as well as from the poverty in which the composer lived.

The next reference to the Mass and Vespers appears in a letter written on September 14, 1610, by the Gonzaga prince, Francesco, to his brother the cardinal. Francesco remarks that Monteverdi is coming to Rome to have some religious compositions published and to present them to the pope.[10] The discrepancy between Francesco's letter and the evidence of Amadino's print, dedicated in Venice on September 1, is probably the result of a misunderstanding on the prince's part. The letter was posted from Pontestura, west of Casale Monferrato, where Francesco was on holiday, and his knowledge of Monteverdi's intentions and of the publication of the Mass and Vespers by Amadino may have been incomplete and imprecise.[11]

When Monteverdi actually departed for Rome is unknown, though it must have been after September 14, since Francesco's letter requests Ferdinando's aid in obtaining a papal audience.[12] There is no evidence that Monteverdi ever had an audience with Pope Paul, but he did make a favorable impression on the Cardinals Montalto and Borghese (the latter the pope's nephew), for they wrote to Duke Vincenzo in Mantua on November 23 and December 4 respectively, describing the composer in glowing terms.[13] If Monteverdi was not still in Rome at the time of these letters, he must have returned to Mantua only shortly before. His next extant letter is dated Mantua, December 28, 1610, and discusses aspects of his trip.[14]

Hans Redlich has advanced the thesis that Francesco's description of Monteverdi's purpose in going to Rome was accurate in all respects and that the dedication date of Amadino's print does not reflect the actual date of issue. Redlich supports his contention with a letter of Monteverdi's apparently dated January 6, 1611, published by Malipiero.[15] This letter was mailed from Venice and presumably shows that Monteverdi had traveled there almost immediately after the December 28 date of the Mantuan letter mentioned above. Redlich assumes that the purpose of this trip was to oversee the Amadino publication, which was arranged only after Monteverdi's failure to get the collection printed in Rome:

> That the first-print could not have been issued during the month of September is proved by the corroborative evidence of a handwritten copy of the Mass which survives in the Biblioteca Apostolica Vaticana (Cappella Sistina No. 107). This was the actual dedication copy presented to Pope Paul V on the occasion of Monteverdi's visit to Rome. That copy was renewed—presumably because of wear and tear owing to repeated use—under the Pontificate of Innozenz [sic] XI and Benedict XIII in 1683 and 1724 respectively. In addition: We know that Monteverdi was back in Mantua by December 28, 1610, proceeding from there hurriedly to Venice from where he wrote a letter on January 6, 1611. What else could have necessitated this hectic journey, coming so soon after the return from Rome, but the pending

publication in Venice of his sacred music of 1610? Thus, there is a strong probability
that the Mass (and its companion pieces: The Vespers of the Blessed Virgin and the
two settings of the Magnificat) was only published around New Year 1611. In that
case the Vatican copy would represent an earlier editorial stage of the "Missa". The
fact that it differs in several respects from the version of the first-print can only
underscore that probability.[16]

The letter supposedly placing Monteverdi in Venice at the beginning of
1611 considers the proposed composition of a theatrical work, *Le Nozze di
Tetide, favola Maritima,* which was the subject of a series of exchanges between Monteverdi and the Mantuan court secretary (and librettist of
L'Orfeo), Alessandro Striggio. These letters do not fall in 1611, however,
but between December 1616 and February 1617. Monteverdi's side of the
correspondence is all posted from Venice, since he had already been
employed at San Marco for more than three years. Malipiero uncritically
accepted the year on the January 6 letter without regard to its contents,
although Henri Prunières had earlier noted the discrepancy and assigned the
letter to its proper sequence according to the subject matter.[17] In his recent
edition of the correspondence, De' Paoli has also correctly placed this letter.[18] Redlich's theory is thus lacking foundation. There was no "hectic
journey" to Venice in January of 1611, the Mass and Vespers were indeed
issued in the *Serenissima* on September 1, 1610, and Francesco was simply
mistaken in thinking Monteverdi was seeking a publisher in Rome.

In this light, the preservation of only the Mass in the *Biblioteca Apostolica Vaticana* is of interest. The manuscript copy, as noted above, is without *basso continuo,* since the choir of the *Cappella Sistina* sang without
benefit of organ or other instruments. Either Monteverdi did not personally
offer the Amadino *print* to the pope, even though the entire collection is
dedicated to Paul V, or the copy he presented has vanished. In either event,
the elaborate modern style of the Vespers was completely unsuited to
Roman conservatism and the pope's strong Counter-Reformation attitudes.
In fact, polyphonic Vesper music was confined for the most part to
northern Italy, and comparatively little of it was produced in Rome before
1620. If Monteverdi was indeed seeking a new position in Rome, as both
De' Paoli and Denis Arnold suggest (quite probable in view of Monteverdi's
discontent at Mantua), the Mass would have been an appropriate vehicle of
introduction.[19] The Vespers, however, were much more suited to Venice,
where Monteverdi finally did obtain employment in 1613.[20]

It seems, therefore, that Monteverdi was advertising himself as a composer of sacred music in two musical capitals at once: Rome with the Mass
and Venice with the Vespers. The stylistic dichotomy between the two parts
of the Amadino print reflects the cultural and political differences between
the two cities, which had grown in intensity throughout the sixteenth century and had finally resulted in a papal interdict between 1606 and 1607, im-
posed upon the republic by Monteverdi's dedicatee, Paul V.[21]

Although the reason that two sources for the Mass survive is sufficiently clear, the musical relationship between these sources is not so obvious. Both versions of the work contain errors, and each has better readings than the other in certain passages. In some instances two divergent readings are equally satisfactory. Where there are differences in text underlay, which are at times substantial, the manuscript is almost always superior to the print. A peculiar deviation between the two sources is an interchange of the *Cantus* and *Sextus* parts in the first section of the *Sanctus*. At the *Benedictus* the two parts are once again in agreement in both versions. This reversal of voices has no real bearing on the sonority of the composition, though, since both parts are notated in the C_1 clef, share the same range, and frequently exchange identical material.

The equally good readings of several different passages in the two sources suggest that neither can be considered an original version. The differences may have resulted from corruptions introduced by copyists and typesetters in working from the composer's lost autograph. The copy Monteverdi originally presented to Pope Paul may even have differed in some details from the source used by Amadino in preparing his print. The Vatican version may also have been altered in the process of restoration. It is probable that errors encountered by *Cappella Sistina* singers in the initial manuscript were corrected in the first restoration. On the other hand, new errors may have crept into the restorations through miscopying. Only the superiority of the text underlay argues for the priority of the Vatican manuscript as a source for a modern edition. Even the differences in text underlay reveal nothing about the original relationship between the first Vatican manuscript and the copy given Amadino, however, for Amadino's poor underlay is likely the result of negligence on the part of the typesetter, a not uncommon occurrence in late sixteenth- and early seventeenth-century printed music.

Another feature in which the Vatican and Venetian sources differ is the quotation at the beginning of the Mass of the ten *fughe* from the parodied Gombert motet. The two sequences of motives are not identical, and there are even slight discrepancies in the notation of a few *fughe* (see example 1). The *Fuga prima* is the chief motive of the Mass, and the first two motives in both sources are in the order they appear in Gombert's work, but otherwise the sequences seem to be random. The differences between the manuscript and the print, therefore, have no particular meaning.

The dedication in the two sources is relatively brief in comparison to the lavish encomiums heaped on secular and sacred princes in many publications of the sixteenth and seventeenth centuries.[22] It should be noted, though, that most dedications were addressed to individuals from whom an author had already received patronage or with whom he had had enough contact to justify the hope for future patronage. Many composers, therefore, were more verbose in eulogizing their dedicatees than is Monte-

EXAMPLE 1

verdi in the rather concise, impersonal remarks he addresses to the pope. Aside from the ordinary formulas of praise customary in such prefaces, Monteverdi does make two specific references to himself. One of his purposes in publishing this music, he says, is so that "the mouths of those speaking unjust things against Claudio may be closed."[23] This remark is evidently aimed at Artusi's censure of Monteverdi's contrapuntal skill, about which the composer may still have chafed in 1610.[24] Monteverdi's sensitivity to detractors was apparently of long standing, for he had alluded to his need for protection from "malevolorum linguis" in the dedication of his youthful Sacrae Cantiunculae of 1582.[25] The other personal reference in the 1610 dedication is to his "nocturnal labors," which, if it is not merely a conventional phrase, may be suggestive of the composer's working habits.

Monteverdi's boldness in dedicating his first major collection of sacred music to the pope deserves comment. Although the composer's reputation had undoubtedly been expanding steadily since the late 1590s, beginning in 1600 he found himself the object of calumny and notoriety through the attacks of Artusi. But with the success of *L'Orfeo* in 1607 and *Arianna* in the next year, Monteverdi achieved a degree of fame which must have substantially bolstered his confidence, even if it left him physically exhausted and as penurious as ever. He may have been emboldened to approach the pope not only because of dissatisfaction with his financial condition and the pressures of Mantuan court life, but also because of an increasing awareness of his own reputation and stature. It must have been a grave disappointment that he did not find a position in Rome and was unsuccessful in obtaining the free admission to the papal seminary that he ardently sought for his son Francesco. But these failures ultimately led to his good fortune, for the position he finally attained as *Maestro di Cappella* at San Marco was eminently more suited to his musical and dramatic interests and capabilities than anything Rome could have offered.

ERRORS AND INCONSISTENCIES IN THE PRINT

Errors in Amadino's print may be of three different origins: mistakes by the composer, copying errors in the manuscript from which the printer worked, and misprints resulting from faulty typesetting. Although it is often impossible to determine the source of an error, inconsistencies of notation can at times be traced to the composer, while some specific categories of errors were almost certainly made at either the copying or the typesetting stages.

Examples of the latter are errors in which a repeated or sequential phrase was either omitted or reiterated once too often in a single part-book. This type of mistake evidently resulted from the eyes of the copyist or typesetter moving back and forth from his source to his own work. In returning to the source, his vision may have lighted on the correct passage, but the wrong repetition, yielding one too few or one too many reiterations in his own copy. This is one of the most common types of error in the print, easily emended through comparison with the other part-books.

Another common error is the notation of rhythms in either augmentation or diminution of their proper values. Such flaws occur not only in isolated notes, but also in dotted rhythms; for example, a dotted minim followed by a semiminim may have been inscribed as a dotted semiminim and *fusa* or vice versa. A mistake of this kind could have arisen at any of the three stages of preparation and was probably the result of the composer, copyist, or typesetter establishing an aural image of the rhythm in his mind, but then actually notating it at the wrong level. Once again such errors are easily corrected by analogy with other parts.

Yet another type of error, which probably derives from faulty copying or typesetting, is the misplacement of clefs or melodic figures. Occasionally a melodic figure appears too high or too low by a step or a third. In the latter instance the error may have been the outcome of temporarily thinking in the wrong C clef. The C clefs themselves are sometimes placed incorrectly, especially at the beginning of a new staff.

Misplacement of accidentals also occurs with some frequency. An accidental may be positioned on the wrong line or space or in front of the wrong note, usually the one immediately before or after the appropriate pitch. Because sharps are limited mostly to F, C, and G, and flats to B, E, and an occasional A, errors in placement of accidentals seldom provide difficulties in transcription.

Musica ficta and its relationship to notated accidentals is somewhat more problematic. Accidentals are also treated slightly differently in the Vespers and the Mass. In the Vespers there is normally an accidental before each note requiring alteration except repeated pitches. Consequently, a repeated-note cadential figure may be notated in the following manner:

ILLUSTRATION 1

While this is the general practice in the Vespers, it is not followed with absolute fidelity. But the pattern is clear enough to consider occasional exceptions as anomalies within the general rule. In some instances the cadential leading tone does not carry the appropriate accidental, but its alteration is obvious. In non-cadential passages Monteverdi tends to be careful and precise, especially where uncertainties might otherwise arise.

In the *Missa In illo tempore,* accidentals and *musica ficta* pose many of the same problems encountered in polyphonic works of the sixteenth century. Reversing the notational practice of the Vespers, Monteverdi usually repeats an accidental in front of a reiterated pitch in the Mass (in the polyphonic style repeated notes are much less frequent). Cautionary signs are also used to avoid flatting or sharpening notes that might otherwise be altered in accordance with the normal rules of *musica ficta.* [26] Questions do arise, however, as to how strictly the rules of *ficta* are to apply and to how far an accidental at a cadence should extend backward into the polyphonic texture. In addition, erroneous omissions of accidentals in the Mass are likely to have a greater effect on performance than in the Vespers, since the Mass is more closely tied to the modal scales and more subject to ambiguities of interpretation.

A section from near the beginning of the *Gloria* illustrates the problems of *musica ficta* and the notation of accidentals in the Mass (see example 2). The passage begins with a clearly articulated cadence in C major, but moves in bar 14 toward G major, where Monteverdi has placed a sharp in front of the quarter-note f' in the *Altus*. A firm cadence in G does not actually arrive until bar 16. The sequence in the *Tenor* in bar 15, imitating the *Altus,* should probably also have an f'-sharp, but the descending passing tones in the *Sextus, Altus,* and *Quintus* in bars 14-16 could probably remain unaltered.

These ambiguities continue in the following measures. The extension of G major after bar 16 suggests an f''-sharp in the *Cantus* in bar 17, but the motive there is a direct imitation of the *Sextus* and *Quintus* in bars 15 and 16 where an F-natural seems appropriate. The melodic sequences and G major tonality from bar 17 onward, however, suggest F-sharps throughout, including the neighboring-tone first note of the *Altus* in bar 19, which produces a diminished triad at that point.

From bars 20-23 the employment of *ficta* alterations is more problematic. The middle voices in bar 20 seem to require f'-sharps, thereby forcing one in the organ as well. But as the same sequence continues in bars 21-23, the harmonic movement is toward a deceptive cadence in the key of C major in the second half of bar 23. The full C major cadence is finally reached in bar 24, overlapping with the beginning of the next phrase. This sequence and harmonic direction suggest sharps in bar 21 for the first f' in the *Altus* and f in the *Bassus,* but unaltered F's in the *Sextus* and *Bassus* at the end of the bar. All F's would thereafter remain natural until bar 25, where Monteverdi once again notates an f'-sharp in the *Altus,* signaling movement back toward another G major cadence. The remainder of the passage is then clearly notated through the cadence in bars 27-28. Only the last f' in the *Altus* in bar 25 is left unaltered and probably should remain so because of the brief C major cadence at that point.

This passage demonstrates how complicated the interpretation of *musica ficta* can become in the Mass because of the absence of accidentals. It is fortunate indeed that the use of sharps and flats in the Vespers is much clearer, if not totally unambiguous and free of errors.

Other mistakes in the print affect only individual items in the musical notation. A single note may be incorrectly placed or omitted; an isolated rhythmic value may be faulty; a rest or tie may be missing. Lengthy rests are frequently notated inaccurately, with the total values too small or too large. It is also common for the meter signs ₵ and C to be interchanged. This ambivalence reflects a widespread confusion among printers as to the meaning of the two signs and their relationship to one another. Although theorists are largely in agreement regarding the general tempo relationship between ₵ and C as well as the size of note values appropriate to each, the two are often mixed indiscriminately in late sixteenth- and early seventeenth-century publications. In Amadino's print it is quite common to find a ₵ in one voice conflicting with a C in another.

EXAMPLE 2: *Gloria*

Recognition of categories of errors and their possible origins not only helps clarify questionable or problematic passages, but also can be suggestive about the relationship between the sources and even between individual compositions in the print. Of particular interest are the wide differences in the number of errors among the various pieces in the Vespers. Most of the compositions have what may be termed a "normal" number of mistakes for a publication from this period. The quantity of errors is not excessive, yet there are enough to create occasional transcription problems and to betoken inattentive proofreading at one or more stages of the copying or typesetting process. In contrast to this admittedly vague norm are those pieces with either very few errors or an extraordinarily high proportion of mistakes.

An example of the former is the psalm *Nisi Dominus,* which, despite its thick ten-part texture and great length, reveals only two notational errors. This exceptionally small number indicates that the typesetter had an excellent manuscript copy from which to work. The quality of that copy may in turn be informative about the chronological relationship between *Nisi Dominus* and other pieces in the Vespers, since the almost perfect manuscript evidently resulted from ample opportunity to correct the original score. In other words, *Nisi Dominus* probably underwent rehearsals and performances through which mistakes could be discovered and carefully corrected in a clear, accurate final draft. The psalm *Lauda Jeru-*

salem is almost as remarkable in its accuracy in the print, possibly presupposing the same conditions. If these two psalms were sent to the printer in such excellent copies, it may well be that they were composed somewhat earlier than the other works in the collection, allowing time for rehearsals, performances, and emendations.

This hypothesis correlates with stylistic differences between these two pieces and the other three psalms of the Vespers. With its long-note *cantus firmus* in the two tenors and its strict *coro spezzato* technique, *Nisi Dominus* is certainly the most conservative of all the psalms. *Lauda Jerusalem* is somewhat more flexible and complex, but its scoring, consisting of a tenor surrounded by two three-voice groups continually alternating and overlapping, approximates the *spezzato* style. Like *Nisi Dominus*, the *cantus firmus* is in the tenor, except for the Doxology, although the rhythmic movement of the chant resembles the other psalms in its rapidity.

Both of these pieces, in employing traditional textures and techniques, contrast with the three more modern *concertato* psalms. In addition, neither *Nisi Dominus* nor *Lauda Jerusalem* corresponds to the basic tonal scheme of the Vespers. While Monteverdi's tonal plan cannot be termed systematic, the primary key centers of the Vespers are D major and minor and G major and minor. The first psalm, *Dixit Dominus,* in A minor, is an exception. *Nisi Dominus,* however, is in F major and *Lauda Jerusalem,* although never settling firmly into any tonality, is for the most part in C major with frequent full cadences in A major. *Lauda Jerusalem* is also the only psalm notated in *chiavette* instead of *chiavi naturali.*[27] The evidence of Amadino's print, therefore, coupled with stylistic considerations, suggests that both *Nisi Dominus* and *Lauda Jerusalem* antedated other compositions in the Vespers and are not closely unified in style, technique, and tonality to the other components of the collection.

At the opposite end of the spectrum from *Nisi Dominus* is the immediately following motet, *Audi coelum.* This piece has a bipartite structure: the first section is for two solo tenors in the modern monodic style (the second tenor functions strictly as an echo), while the second section is in six-voice polyphony. *Audi coelum* is replete with errors. In view of the accuracy with which *Nisi Dominus* and *Lauda Jerusalem* were printed, it seems improbable that the blame should be laid on a careless or overly hasty typesetter. More likely is that the motet had been completed only shortly before its publication, perhaps had never been performed, and was submitted to the printer in a faulty, slipshod copy.

Of particular note in *Audi coelum* is a melisma in the *Tenor* and *Quintus* part-books that differs rhythmically and melodically from the version in the *Bassus Generalis,* where the two voices are reproduced above the bass line. Most of the melismas are identical between the part-books and the *partitura,* but in this instance there are two different, but equally good readings

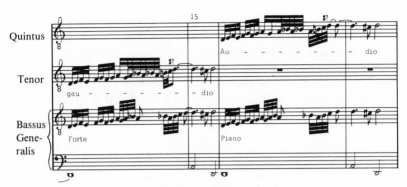

EXAMPLE 3. *Audi coelum*

(see example 3). The only factor suggesting the priority of the *Bassus Generalis* version is the rhythmic consistency between the first melisma and its echo. The *Tenor* and *Quintus* part-books differ slightly at this point.[28]

Similar discrepancies between the *Bassus Generalis* and the vocal part-books exist at the conclusion of the *Deposuit* in the *Magnificat à 6* (see example 4). This time the *Bassus Generalis* is definitely a better version, for the part-books have a major break in rhythmic motion in the antepenultimate bar.[29]

EXAMPLE 4. *Magnificat à 6: Deposuit*

In other instances where the part-books and the *Bassus Generalis* diverge in their notation of the same material, the *Bassus Generalis* is usually the superior reading. This observation, coupled with the unique performance rubrics in the *partitura,* illustrates the greater significance of the *Bassus Generalis* to the composer and performers. For the organist, who may well have been the musical director for rehearsals and performance, the *partitura* served as a guide, apprising him of some or all of the upper parts of a composition. Where a separate *maestro di cappella* was responsible for preparation of the work, the *Bassus Generalis* could have served additionally as a conductor's short score. It is only natural, therefore, that the *Bassus Generalis* would contain information and performance directions not in the other books and might have been prepared with greater care before being given to the printer.

EXAMPLE 5: *Nisi Dominus*

An understanding of the types of errors in the print can also assist in developing better readings than have heretofore appeared in modern editions for certain faulty passages. A case in point is the conclusion of *Nisi Dominus,* where one of the psalm's two errors occurs. The passage is notated in the part-books as in example 5. Several editors of the Vespers have emended this passage identically (see example 6). This correction postulates two simultaneous misprints in the *Altus* and *Sextus* part-books in a composition that to this point has witnessed only one other mistake.[30] A simpler and more logical assumption is that there is only one error, in the *Quintus* of the first choir (*Altus* part-book) in bar 211. Here there is an extraneous semibreve *c,* occasioned by one too many repetitions of that pitch (albeit all in different rhythmic values). Elimination of this semibreve produces a slightly altered conclusion to the psalm (see example 7).[31]

EXAMPLE 6. *Nisi Dominus*

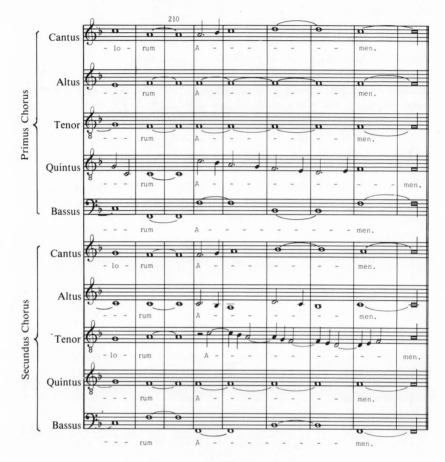

EXAMPLE 7. *Nisi Dominus*

An error of omission, one of the few faulty readings in *Lauda Jerusalem,* has also been resolved by editors of the Vespers without reference to either the passage in which it occurs or the types of errors a copyist or typesetter is likely to make. The passage in the part-books reads as in example 8. Modern editors have filled in the missing pitches in the *Bassus Generalis* by supplying root-position notes for each change of chord (see example 9). But by analogy with the next two bars, the *Bassus Generalis* should double alternately the two bass voices as in example 10. This resolution of the gap sheds light on how it originated. The melodic motive of the *Bassus Generalis* in bars 153-154 is simply a reiteration of the one in bar 152, and either the copyist or the typesetter simply overlooked the repetition in preparing his version.[32]

EXAMPLE 8. *Lauda Jerusalem*

EXAMPLE 9

EXAMPLE 10

A similar mistake of omission arises in *Laetatus sum* in the *Tenor,* where an entire minim beat is missing (see example 11). Editors have assumed that the error lies in the absence of a later rest, which has been added in various places in different editions (see example 12).[33] However, this assumption inevitably forces parallel unisons between the *Tenor* and *Quintus,* regardless

EXAMPLE 11. *Laetatus sum*

EXAMPLE 12. *Laetatus sum*

of where the rest is positioned (see example 13). Denis Stevens noticed this difficulty in preparing his version of the Vespers, and therefore transposed the *Tenor* in the first half of bar 154 of example 13 downward by a third (see example 14).[34] The transposition provides acceptable counterpoint between the *Tenor* and *Quintus*, but creates an octave doubling of the leading-tone *f'*-sharp of the *Sextus* and fails to resolve it in the *Tenor*, leaping upward instead to the following *d'*. Stevens's solution presumes either a compositional error or a temporary misreading of the clef in the copying or typesetting of this passage. A much simpler explanation is that the eye of the copyist or typesetter merely skipped over a beat in the sequence and omitted four notes from the *Tenor*, producing the gap seen in example 11. By observing the *Quintus,* which the *Tenor* imitates precisely until just before the end of the phrase, it is apparent that the *Tenor* should read as in example 15. Further corroboration is provided by the *Cantus*, which is in imitation of the *Tenor* and concords precisely with the emendation suggested here.[35]

EXAMPLE 13. *Laetatus sum*

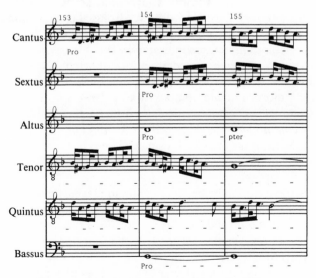

EXAMPLE 14. *Laetatus sum:* Stevens edition

EXAMPLE 15. *Laetatus sum*

THE *BASSUS GENERALIS* AND PERFORMANCE PRACTICE

The greatest ambiguities and problems of interpretation in the Mass and Vespers emerge from the *Bassus Generalis*. In contrast to many contemporary publications, this part is not labelled *Basso per l'organo* or *Partitura per l'organo,* but quite literally, "general bass." The role of this bass and the ways in which the part-book can be utilized involve fundamental issues of performance practice, many aspects of which Monteverdi has deliberately left unspecified, enabling the music to be performed in various manners under varying circumstances.[36] The two different sources of the Mass illustrate this flexibility, since the Vatican version has no instrumental bass at all, in keeping with the previously mentioned tradition of the Sistine Chapel.

The *Bassus Generalis* is primarily for organ, as demonstrated by detailed organ registrations in the two *Magnificat*s and by the *partitura* format of numerous pieces, where the continuo player is provided with vocal or instrumental parts in addition to his own bass line.

The organ, of course, was the appropriate keyboard instrument for sacred music, although harpsichords were also used in the Church on occasion.[37] In addition, a variety of plucked instruments could furnish the continuo for few-voiced motets, as indicated by the title pages of many sacred collections and by contemporary descriptions of actual performances.[38] Instruments other than the organ, therefore, may well have supported Monteverdi's more intimate compositions, *Nigra sum, Pulchra es, Duo Seraphim*, and *Audi coelum*, particularly if they were to be *"ad Principum Cubicula accommodata"* as described on the title page. A change of continuo instruments in the course of a single piece is also not out of the question, especially in the *concertato* psalms where radically different styles and textures are juxtaposed.[39]

The score for the organist or other continuo player is notated differently from one composition to the next. In the *Missa In illo tempore* the part is labelled *Basso Continuo* and consists mostly of the simple organ bass line.[40] But in the *Crucifixus,* composed for only the four upper voices instead of the normal six, Monteverdi provides a complete, four-part organ *partitura*. Does this *partitura* signify any change in the manner of performance?

The reduction of the texture to four high voices for the *Crucifixus* was a widespread tradition in late sixteenth- and early seventeenth-century polyphonic masses, and after the turn of the century it was not unusual for this thinner texture to be notated fully in the organ *partitura*.[41] The purpose of this procedure is not entirely clear. It is presumed that an organist would have had to write out some kind of *partitura* from the organ bass and part-books of a polyphonic composition in order to accompany it satisfactorily. Numerous seventeenth-century writers attest to the necessity for making such an organ score, and the *partitura* by Lorenzo Tonelli is a specific instance of this practice with regard to Monteverdi's Mass. Some publications spared the organist the extra trouble by printing a full *partitura* or a reduced score with at least one upper part.[42] Perhaps Amadino did not find it too expensive to provide a *partitura* of the relatively short *Crucifixus* in order to relieve the organist from writing out his own score for that portion of the *Credo*. The amount of copying spared, however, is minimal in relation to the entire Mass. It is more likely that the solemnity of the *Crucifixus,* signaled by the reduced texture and lighter choral sound, was to be emphasized by as faithful a doubling of the vocal polyphony as the organist could achieve. In other sections employing the full choir, the organist could only play whatever parts of the texture conveniently adapted to his fingers and keyboard technique.

The full *partitura* in the *Crucifixus* may also indicate a change in other aspects of accompaniment. It is well known that instruments were often used to double the vocal parts of polyphonic sacred music in the sixteenth and seventeenth centuries, and there is evidence of extensive use of instruments in the ducal church of Santa Barbara in Mantua.[43] If other instruments in addition to the organ participated in a performance of the Mass, they may have ceased during the reduced *Crucifixus,* leaving the entire accompaniment to the organist alone. The organ, in the absence of other doubling, would have needed to reproduce faithfully the complete polyphonic texture.

In the Vespers the treatment of the continuo is more complicated and varied than in the Mass. Because of the rhythmic diversity of the upper parts in many of the pieces, Monteverdi often furnishes at least one of these parts as a guide in the *Bassus Generalis*. The respond *Domine ad adiuvandum,* for example, has the topmost instrumental line notated over the bass. The rhythm of the voices in this piece can be determined only through the *Bassus Generalis,* since in the part-books the *falsobordone* setting of the text entails unrhythmicized long notes. Only in the *partitura* is the *falsobordone* given a rhythmic shape, with the text underlaid beneath the organ bass and the syllables distributed according to their appropriate rhythmic declamation.

Monteverdi uses two separate approaches to the organ notation of the five psalms. Three of the psalms, *Dixit Dominus, Nisi Dominus,* and *Lauda*

Jerusalem, are represented simply by their bass lines. *Laudate pueri* and *Laetatus sum,* on the other hand, also have two other staves because of the virtuoso melismas integral to their structure. The first three psalms conceivably could be accompanied by the organist without the aid of a *partitura,* since their textures are homophonically derived and their rhythmic movement is straightforward. The latter two works, however, include *passaggi* in rapid rhythms for virtuoso singers, undoubtedly soloists. These melismas may necessitate both flexibility in rhythm and changes in tempo. Since the organist plays sustained chords in these passages, Monteverdi supplies him with cues in the form of whatever upper parts can assist in following the rhythm and harmony. Most often these added parts consist of the top two lines in any given section, but not always. Monteverdi's choice is dictated by the information most useful to the organist, so inner parts that reveal the harmony more clearly or that contain rhythmic motion difficult to follow may be included in place of the topmost lines.

Performance rubrics for some of the psalms are an additional ingredient exclusive to the *Bassus Generalis* part-book. *Dixit Dominus* is headed by an instruction that the instrumental *ritornelli* may be omitted *ad libitum: "Li Ritornelli si possano sonare & anco tralasciare secondo il volere."* This leaves open the use of instruments according to their availability and their appropriateness for a particular performance. The psalm *Laudate pueri* carries the rubric *"à 8. voci sole nel Organo."* This caption not only calls for solo voices instead of the choir, but possibly also signifies the absence of accompanying instruments, which could easily overwhelm the soloists. The other three psalms are marked simply with the number of voice parts and are presumably to be sung chorally. Nevertheless, the virtuoso passagework in *Laetatus sum* certainly demands solo voices at those moments. The necessity for soloists would have been obvious without rubrics to seventeenth-century musicians from the *passaggi* themselves.

The hymn *Ave maris stella* is another piece provided merely with the bass line in the *Bassus Generalis.* Once again it is only through rubrics in this part-book that performance by soloists of the fourth, fifth, and sixth verses is specified. There is no indication, as in *Dixit Dominus,* that the instrumental *ritornelli* are optional, but if Monteverdi intended to make the strictly liturgical parts of the Vespers performable with or without instruments, then it may be assumed that these *ritornelli* are *ad libitum* as well.

The *Sonata sopra Sancta Maria,* with its soprano *cantus firmus* intoned over a very large instrumental sonata, has a complicated continuo notation. The *Cantus,* which sings only intermittently, is equipped with its own continuo in the *Cantus* part-book itself. This continuo is an exact duplicate of the organ bass in the *Bassus Generalis* except for a few minor rhythmic discrepancies. Its function is to act as a guide for the soprano or sopranos (there is no indication in the part-book or *Bassus Generalis* whether or not a

soloist is required) in much the same way that vocal parts are at times furnished to assist the organist. With this continuo part in view, the *Cantus* can
follow the progress of the *Sonata* and enter at the appropriate points.[44]

In the *Bassus Generalis* the organ part of the *Sonata* consists primarily of
a single bass line. Part way through the composition, however, when paired
violins begin virtuoso *passaggi* similar to those in the vocal portions of the
Vespers, a second continuo line is added. This second line is not intended as
merely a visual aid to the organist, since it does not reproduce the rapid
rhythms of the violins. Instead, both the bass line and this second part
outline in semiminims the notes ornamented more elaborately in the violins
and later in the *cornetti* (see example 16). In this instance the organ is obviously not to play harmony, but to double in simpler rhythm the underlying melodic movement of the instruments. This heterophonic doubling continues as long as there is no bass part supporting the virtuoso pair. As soon
as a lower instrumental part enters, the top line of the organ score rests
while the bottom line drops down to double the supporting instrument.
When another high-instrument duet begins and the lower instruments exit,
the organ resumes its own high-register doubling of the duet. This procedure ends quite suddenly the last time that lower instruments enter. At
that point the upper continuo line ceases abruptly and disappears altogether
from the *Bassus Generalis* part-book, since the lower instruments continue
through the remainder of the *Sonata.*

The four motets, *Nigra sum, Pulchra es, Duo Seraphim,* and *Audi
coelum*, all have complete vocal parts above the bass in the *partitura*. These
vocal scores are essential for the continuo player not only to follow the complex rhythms of the singers, but also to adjust to the elasticity of rhythm
and tempo normally expected of soloists. Of the four pieces, only *Audi
coelum* is actually designated for solo voice in the *Bassus Generalis,* the
rubrics for the others merely indicating the number of voice parts. Nevertheless, the style of these pieces, derived from monody and virtuoso duets,

EXAMPLE 16. *Sonata sopra Sancta Maria*

unquestionably requires soloists.[45] The annotation for *Audi coelum* reads in full, *"prima ad una voce sola, poi nella fine à 6 voci."* This caption was obviously necessitated by the structure of the piece, which advances to six parts after the initial solo with echo. The specification of a single voice points up the contrast with the six-part section, which probably should be sung by a choir.

In the first section the melismatic echoes, assigned in the part-books to the *Quintus,* are notated in the *Bassus Generalis* on the same staff as the tenor voice. Each melisma is marked *forte* and each echo *piano,* instructing the continuo player to adjust his dynamics accordingly.

When *Audi coelum* expands to six parts in a polyphonic style, the voices are dropped from the *Bassus Generalis* except for those passages where the *Tenor* and *Quintus* re-enter with melismas. Presuming that a chorus is to be used for the polyphonic section, these melismas should revert to soloists because of their affinity with the earlier part of the motet and their reprise of the echo technique.

In *Nigra sum* and *Pulchra es* there are some curious discrepancies between the notation of the voices in the part-books and in the *Bassus Generalis.* At the beginning of *Pulchra es,* the top line of the three-staff continuo score is an ornamental counterpoint to the voice rather than a duplication of it (see example 17). In fact, this top line is nearly identical to the *Sextus,* or second soprano, which first enters several bars later (see example 18). This brief counterpoint, apparently to be performed by the continuo, raises the issue of how closely the continuo player is to follow the upper parts printed in the *Bassus Generalis* in this and the other motets. Is he merely to play a simple underlying harmony, or should he actually double most of the vocal lines? The testimony of early seventeenth-century composers and theorists is contradictory on this point. Some writers suggest that

EXAMPLE 17. *Pulchra es*

solo vocal lines be supported by the upper part of the accompaniment, while others are opposed to doubling of the topmost voice.[46] In virtuoso motets like those in the Vespers, it is often impractical for a single player to duplicate the ornamentation and complex rhythm of the voices. Yet the continuo player may have been expected to double the melodic outline of the vocal parts in a heterophonic manner similar to that which Monteverdi himself notates in the *Sonata sopra Sancta Maria*. In the duet *Pulchra es,* the character and relationship of the parts are such that a cembalist or organist *could* double the voices almost verbatim. Whether or not the continuo supports the singers with doubling or partial doubling may also depend on the continuo instrument chosen, the strength of the voices and the size and acoustics of the room in which the work is to be performed. As will be seen below in the discussion of melody instruments, it might also prove feasible to double the voices with separate instruments apart from the continuo.

The reason for Monteverdi's counterpoint at the beginning of *Pulchra es* probably lies in the thinness of the texture at that point, where the solo *Cantus* sings slow, sustained tones. In order to alleviate the rhythmic inactivity of the voice, a more lively counterpoint is given the continuo, the same variant of the *Cantus* part that will soon appear in the *Sextus*. The ornamented version in the continuo also suggests that the singer should not improvise embellishments during this passage, for the ornamental role is clearly assigned to the supporting instrument.

In *Nigra sum* the differences between the tenor and *Bassus Generalis* part-books mostly involve vocal dotted rhythms, which are notated evenly in the continuo score (see example 19). Monteverdi is inconsistent in this piece, accurately duplicating some of the vocal rhythms in the continuo part while altering others. Where the continuo is at odds with the voice, the *Bassus*

EXAMPLE 18. *Pulchra es*

EXAMPLE 19. *Nigra sum*

Generalis is merely a simplification of the rhythm, which does not affect the player's ability to follow the soloist. These inconsistencies and discrepancies between the two parts may be attributable either to carelessness in copying or to changes Monteverdi decided to make in the part-book version after the *Bassus Generalis* had been completed. If changes were made, perhaps even at the last minute before publication, corresponding alterations in the *Bassus Generalis* were neglected.

The most elaborate performance directions in the Vespers are contained in the organ scores for the two *Magnificats*. Registration for the organist is specified in detail, in some cases even changing in the middle of individual verses.[47] These annotations are carefully considered with regard to expressive effects and the sonorities of voices and *obbligato* instruments. The *Bassus Generalis* comprises primarily the single bass line, its registration, indications of the vocal scoring, and occasional references to musical style (*echo, dialogo,* etc.). In the *Quia respexit* of the *Magnificat à 7* there is even an instruction for the *obbligato* instruments to play as loudly as possible, and in the same segment of the *Magnificat à 6,* the voice is directed to sing loudly. In some instances rubrics specify solo voices, while in others the virtuoso style obviously requires soloists and no rubric is necessary.

In several *Magnificat* sections the organist is instructed to play slowly because of rapid movement or echo technique in the upper parts.[48] In these passages Monteverdi expects the organist to get along without the vocal lines in view, and the rhythmic regularity of their melismas would indeed make that possible. In the *Deposuit* of both *Magnificats* and the *Gloria Patri* of the *Magnificat à 7,* however, the *Bassus Generalis* incorporates a full score of the instrumental and vocal parts. In all three instances the voices and instruments have such lively, rhythmically complex echoes and imitations that the upper parts are essential for the organist to keep track of the other performers. A full *partitura* might also have proved helpful in those sections where the organist is directed to play slowly, but Monteverdi has provided the full score in the *Magnificats* only where absolutely necessary.

Although the role of the organ in the Vespers seems sufficiently clear, both from Monteverdi's *Bassus Generalis* and what is known of early *Seicento* continuo practice, the question still remains as to what part other instruments might have played in performances of the music. *Obbligato* instruments are specified in the *Sonata sopra Sancta Maria* and the *Magnificat à 7*. Instrumental *ritornelli* separate several verses of the hymn. Optional instrumental accompaniment and instrumental *ritornelli* appear in the respond and *Dixit Dominus*. Are instruments to be employed elsewhere in the Vespers as well? Amadino's print offers no additional information. However, the *obbligato* and *ad libitum* orchestration in five of the pieces, the frequent use of instruments in the Gonzaga church of Santa Barbara and other north Italian churches, and contemporary accounts of improvising instruments all strongly suggest instrumental participation in other portions of the Vespers. Mention has already been made of continuo instruments that could possibly have replaced the organ, especially in the four motets. In the hymn and psalms, with the exception of *Laudate pueri à 8 voci sole nel Organo,* the thick textures and full choral sonorities may have been supported by multiple foundation instruments.[49] To the organ could have been added *chitarroni* or the low strings and brass that so firmly bolster the respond. If so, the number of foundation instruments would likely have depended upon the size of the choir and the dimensions and acoustical properties of the room in which a performance was to take place.

The middle and high register instruments named in the print might similarly have doubled voices in the Mass, the psalms, and the hymn. Except for the polyphonic section of *Audi coelum,* doubling in the motets is less plausible because of the delicacy of the solo voices and the imperative for expressive freedom—Caccini's *nobile sprezzatura*.[50] Doubling would be more feasible in *Pulchra es* and *Duo Seraphim* than in the other motets, since in these two pieces the voices must adhere to a regular beat sufficiently to sing simultaneous melismas. The addition of instruments, however, might tend to overburden the vocal sonority. Nevertheless, delicate doubling with flutes or *pifare* might prove acceptable in *Pulchra es*. A recent recording of the Vespers doubles the voices effectively in *Duo Seraphim* at the climactic points where the text reads *"plena est omnis terra gloria eius."*[51] Seventeenth-century sources are either silent or vague on the use of doubling instruments in few-voiced motets, offering little in the way of concrete guidelines.[52]

As with the motets, doubling of voices in the *passaggi* of the psalms seems unlikely, though not out of the question. These rhythmically even melismas are of a type often encountered in instrumental as well as vocal music of the early *Seicento,* and coordination of several steadily flowing parts is not overly difficult. The recording of the Vespers noted above employs such doubling successfully in *Laetatus sum*. However, the instrumental doubling of the melismas in this performance does have the effect of decreasing the difference in sonority and character between these solo passages and the other, choral parts of the psalm where instrumental doubling is also used.

In the *Magnificat*s it is highly unlikely that the solo voices would have been doubled *ad libitum*. The *Magnificat à 6* is expressly designed to be performed without instrumental participation, while the extensive orchestration of the *Magnificat à 7* consists entirely of *obbligati* and explicitly specified doublings in the opening and closing full-choir sections. Doubling of the voices in the segments for soloists would destroy the sensitive balance Monteverdi has established between vocal and instrumental sonorities. Perhaps in the polyphonic dialogue, *Et misericordia,* instrumental doubling would be acceptable, but care would have to be taken since Monterverdi calls for *"6 voci sole."* It may even be that *voci sole* refers not only to solo voices but also to voices alone, i.e., without instrumental participation.[53]

In early seventeenth-century vocal music, melody instruments served an even broader purpose than merely doubling voices in the middle and upper registers. According to Agazzari and other sources, instruments often engaged in improvisation as well.[54] The agility of early Baroque violins, *flauti,* and *cornetti* was both a temptation and an invitation to the improvisation of melodic lines and ornaments around the basic notes of the choir or instrumental *ritornelli*. In fact, in those portions of the Vespers where the instruments are not already provided with *passaggi,* improvisation was very likely a part of seventeenth-century performances. The *quantity* of improvisation, however, is the chief issue, and in this regard the Vespers should be approached with two specific cautions.

First, elaborate improvisation is probably more appropriate to purely instrumental passages, such as *ritornelli,* than to sections with large vocal forces. Too much ornamentation in the latter could well obscure the already dense vocal textures, producing contrapuntal confusion. The *ritornelli,* on the other hand, are notated comparatively simply and may gain from tasteful embellishment.

Second, the very explicitness of Monteverdi's orchestration and ornamentation should warn against excessive improvisation. Monteverdi was much more precise and detailed in such matters than any of his contemporaries, and this care bespeaks a shying away from improvisation toward greater control on the part of the composer over the smaller aspects of performance. Monteverdi was leery of abandoning too many details of execution to the judgment of singers, instrumentalists, and *maestri di cappella*. He consequently included many specific performance instructions, including ornamentation, himself.

This argument applies no less to vocal than to instrumental improvisation. The number of treatises describing the art of vocal embellishment in the sixteenth and early seventeenth centuries is impressive and testifies to a widespread tradition.[55] Yet many composers complained of tasteless ornamentation by virtuosi more concerned with projecting their own fame than the qualities of the music.[56] Monteverdi was scarcely adverse to embellishment, but even more than with instruments he notated vocal ornamentation in minute detail. Amadino's print gives the appearance of a more elaborate vocal style than any publication of psalms or motets from that period, yet many pieces by other composers might actually have been sung almost as ornately as Monteverdi's Vespers. The difference lies in notation versus improvisation, with Monteverdi choosing to exert control over ornamentation, to indicate it himself. Monteverdi takes exactly the opposite approach from Caccini, who leaves his melodies in *Le Nuove Musiche* relatively unadorned but attaches a lengthy preface describing appropriate methods of embellishment and expression.

None of this implies that vocal improvisation is to be abjured altogether in the Mass and Vespers. Especially in the motets, small additional embellishments might be suitable and within the bounds of propriety. In the larger choral works cadential ornaments would certainly be appropriate and perhaps a modest amount of other improvisation as well, but in any of the compositions elaborate ornamentation beyond what Monteverdi has specified would defeat the very purpose of his notation.

In a summary overview of the *Bassus Generalis,* the most striking feature is Monteverdi's extraordinary care in supplying performance information and instructions. As with vocal ornamentation, Monteverdi attempts to exercise his authority over as many aspects of execution as practical. Practicality is also at the heart of the scoring in the *partitura,* for Monteverdi seeks always to furnish the organist and/or other continuo players with as much information as necessary to fulfill their roles. His choice of parts for inclusion in the *Bassus Generalis* is ingenious in its variety, purposefulness, and simplicity. The *Bassus Generalis* was obviously prepared with painstaking attention to its various functions, and through it we have much more precise ideas about suitable ways to perform the music than in the vast majority of publications of the early *Seicento.*

Before closing this discussion of performance practice in the Mass and Vespers, the issue of *chiavette* must also be considered. The Mass, *Lauda Jerusalem*, and the two *Magnificats* are all notated in the high clefs, or *chiavette.*[57] Studies have shown convincingly that high *chiavette* often indicated downward transposition by a fourth or some other interval in actual performance, depending on the tuning of accompanying instruments and the ranges of available voices.[58] Because pitch was not absolute in the modern sense and was fixed only by the instruments at hand, transposition by the continuo player was frequently necessary to accommodate voices. If the normal series of clefs would have required more than one ledger line in the vocal parts, *chiavette* were often used instead to facilitate notation and reading. The *chiavette* thus produce the impression of a higher register than was actually intended to be sung. By transposition downward the organist set a lower standard of pitch for the voices, the degree of transposition depending on the tuning of the organ. Most often the high *chiavette* seem to have denoted transposition by a fourth.[59]

That the practice of transposition is applicable to Monteverdi's publication of 1610 is proved by the organ *partitura* of the Mass by Lorenzo Tonelli preserved at Brescia and briefly described at the beginning of this essay. Tonelli's *partitura* comprises a full score incorporating all voice parts plus the organ bass, but with everything transposed down a fourth. The *partitura* is therefore in G major, the same tonality as several other compositions in the print.[60]

A comparison of the notated ranges of the voice parts of those compositions in *chiavi naturali* with the Mass in *chiavette* illustrates the higher *notated* register of the Mass:[61]

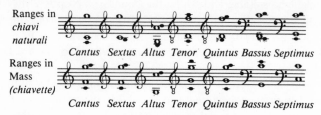

ILLUSTRATION 2

In Tonelli's transposition the voices of the Mass actually sound slightly *lower* than in the pieces with *chiavi naturali:*

ILLUSTRATION 3

While *D* may appear as a rather low note for basses (though certainly not out of the bass range), the absolute pitch varied from organ to organ, and from all indications was somewhat higher than modern pitch.[62] At the top of the untransposed bass range (illustration 2), the *e'* is at the upper extremity for most singers and would probably be out of reach when adjusted to the pitch standards of the seventeenth century. Tonelli's transposition places this note in a more practical register.

At the other end of the gamut, the *Cantus* and *Sextus* are notated in *chiavette* as high as *a"*. This is the highest practical note for boy sopranos in modern pitch and would exceed that maximum when adjusted even higher.

Transposition by a fourth, however, brings this note well within a usable range.

In Tonelli's transposition the *Altus* falls more within the range of a modern tenor and might well have been sung in Monteverdi's day by tenors using *falsetto* to encompass the upper fourth or fifth.[63] The *Tenor* and *Quintus* similarly approximate a modern baritone, with the upper part of the *Tenor* again requiring *falsetto*.

By analogy with the Mass, the psalm *Lauda Jerusalem* could likewise be transposed a fourth downward. The notated ranges of the voices are as follows:

Cantus   Sextus   Altus I Altus II   Tenor   Bassus I Bassus II

ILLUSTRATION 4

Transposition would not only return the voices to manageable registers, but would also bring *Lauda Jerusalem* within the circle of keys of most of the other compositions in the print, aside from the anomalous *Nisi Dominus*.

Clefs in the *Magnificat*s are a more complicated problem. It was customary in the early seventeenth century to notate high instrumental parts in the G clef without denoting transposition. The treble clef was simply more convenient for accommodating the higher registers that instruments could play. Consequently, in the *Sonata sopra Sancta Maria* all the higher instrumental parts are written in G clefs, while the normal tenor and bass clefs are used for the lower instruments and a C_1 clef for the vocal *cantus firmus*. Mixed clefs are also in evidence in *Domine ad adiuvandum*. Here the high and mid-range instruments are notated in G, C_1, and C_3 clefs, while the lower instruments are in tenor and bass clefs. The vocal parts all utilize the *chiavi naturali*. The instrumental *ritornelli* in *Dixit Dominus* and *Ave maris stella*, on the other hand, are fully integrated with the voices in the partbooks and therefore retain the normal clefs.

In the two *Magnificat*s, *chiavette* are found in all parts. Could these pieces also have been transposed down a fourth? The notated high registers in the canticles are not so troublesome as in the Mass and *Lauda Jerusalem*, since most of the sections with a high tessitura are designed for solo virtuosi. In the choral sections high registers are infrequent, though not altogether absent. Transposition would bring the *Magnificat*s into the same vocal ranges as the transposed Mass and *Lauda Jerusalem*, and is perhaps justified for that reason. The resultant change of register would also be feasible for all the *obbligato* instruments in the *Magnificat à 7*.[64] Additionally, transposition would shift the tonality to D minor, the same tonic as the opening respond. As balanced as an opening and closing on D may seem, however, Monteverdi's approach to tonality in the Vespers is insufficiently systematic to imply that tonal symmetry is a primary consideration, especially since the *Magnificats*' notated G minor accords with several other compositions in the print.

The issue of transposition in the Mass, *Lauda Jerusalem,* and the *Magnificats* is not to be settled by any hard and fast rule. Sufficient evidence has been marshalled to warrant transposition of all four pieces, but instability of pitch in the seventeenth century may have allowed local conditions and resources to hold sway in determining the interval of transposition and even whether or not to transpose at all. With modern fixed pitch, lower than in the seventeenth century, transposition downward by a fourth forces the basses into a register at least as uncomfortable as the high range demanded of sopranos when the score is performed as notated. The vocal sonority of most modern performances is also significantly altered through the replacement of boy sopranos and male altos by female voices. Thus changes in pitch and singers have alleviated some of the conditions that led to transposition in Monteverdi's time. The absence of a truly systematic tonal plan in the Vespers leaves modern performers free to make choices according to the same criteria as in the seventeenth century: the instrumental and vocal resources at hand. Where practical, transposition by a fourth might have a greater air of authenticity and would reproduce Monteverdi's original tonal relationships, but it is by no means essential.

NOTES

1. For the full title of the collection, see the Introduction, p. 6, note 7. The locations of copies of the part-books are listed in Claudio Sartori, *Bibliografia della Musica Strumentale Italiana* (Florence: Leo S. Olschki, 1952-1968), vol. I, p. 173, and vol. II, pp. 53-54. Sartori's listings, complete with mistakes, are reproduced in *International Inventory of Musical Sources: Einzeldrucke vor 1800* (Kassel: Bärenreiter, 1976), vol. VI, p. 10. According to Sartori, the University Library in Wroclaw, Poland, possesses a copy of the *Cantus, Altus, Bassus, Septimus,* and *Bassus Generalis.* However, according to Emil Bohn, *Bibliographie der Musik-Druckwerke bis 1700* (Berlin: Commissions-Verlag von Albert Cohn, 1883; reprint edition Hildesheim: Georg Olms, 1969), p. 288, a complete copy of the work is in the Stadtbibliothek in Wroclaw. My own microfilm is from the University Library and contains the *Cantus, Altus, Tenor, Bassus,* and *Septimus.* This particular copy contains handwritten corrections, *musica ficta,* and Arabic numerals indicating the lengths of rests and long notes.

2. No documentary evidence exists on Lorenzo Tonelli. I am most grateful to Prof. Giovanni Bignami of Brescia for checking local archives and documents in search of information. The paleography of Tonelli's *partitura* places it in the late seventeenth or early eighteenth century. I wish to express my gratitude to Prof. Anne Schnoebelen for assistance in examining a microfilm copy of the *partitura* and estimating its date.

3. The letter is printed as No. 11 in G. Francesco Malipiero, *Claudio Monteverdi* (Milan: Fratelli Treves Editori, 1929), pp. 147-149. The dating of this letter and its repercussions will be discussed below.

4. Some confusion exists on the precise dating of this letter. Davari and De' Paoli give July 16, while Vogel dates it July 26. See Stefano Davari, *Notizie biografiche del destinto Maestro di Musica Claudio Monteverdi* (Mantua: G. Mondovi, 1885), p. 23; Domenico De' Paoli, *Claudio Monteverdi* (Milan: Editore Ulrico Hoepli, 1945), p. 159; and Emil Vogel, "Claudio Monteverdi," *Vierteljahrsschrift für Musikwissenschaft* 3 (1887): 430.

5. "Monteverdi is having printed an *a cappella* Mass for six voices, of much study and labor, since he was obliged to manipulate continually, in every note through all the parts, always further strengthening, the eight motives that are in the motet *In illo tempore* of Gombert. And he is also having printed together [with it] some Vesper psalms of the Virgin with various and diverse manners of invention and harmony, and everything over a *cantus firmus,* with the intention of coming to Rome this autumn to dedicate them to His Holiness. He is also in the midst of preparing a group of madrigals for five voices, which will consist of three laments: that of Arianna, still with its usual soprano, the lament of Leandro and Hero by Marini, the third, given him by His Highness, about a shepherd whose nymph has died. The words [are] by the son of Count Lepido Agnelli on the death of the little Roman [the singer Caterina Martinella]." Vogel, "Claudio Monteverdi," p. 430.

6. These are the cycles *Lamento d'Arianna* and *Lagrime d'Amante al Sepolcro dell'Amata.*

7. Excerpts in English translation are found in Oliver Strunk, *Source Readings in Music History* (New York: W. W. Norton & Company, Inc., 1950), pp. 393-404. The polemics between Artusi and Monteverdi, lasting until 1608, are discussed in Claude V. Palisca, "The Artusi-Monteverdi Controversy," in *The Monteverdi Companion,* ed. Denis Arnold and Nigel Fortune (London: Faber and Faber, 1968), pp. 133-166.

8. Monteverdi's letter is dated December 2, 1608. An English translation by Denis Arnold and Nigel Fortune is in *The Monteverdi Companion,* pp. 26-29. Monteverdi's father, Baldassare, also wrote two letters to the Duke and Duchess of Mantua in the fall of 1608 seeking his son's release from ducal service. See Domenico De' Paoli, *Claudio Monteverdi: Lettere, Dediche e Prefazioni* (Rome: Edizioni de Santis, 1973), pp. 30 and 33. The political circumstances surrounding this wedding are documented in Stuart Reiner, "La vag'Angioletta (and others)," *Analecta Musicologica* 14 (1974): 26-88. See also chapter III, note 1, of this volume.

9. Pierre Tagmann has speculated that composition of the Vespers was stimulated by the birth of the Duke's granddaughter, Maria, on July 29, 1609, and that portions of the Vespers may have been performed on August 15 or September 8, 1609, both feasts of the Virgin. There survive letters from Monteverdi to Alessandro Striggio, however, dated Cremona, August 24, 1609, and September 10, 1609. Both the dates and the contents of these letters render Tagmann's speculations impossible. See Pierre Tagmann, "The Palace Church of Santa Barbara in Mantua, and Monteverdi's Relationship to its Liturgy," in *Festival Essays for Pauline Alderman,* ed. Burton L. Karson (Brigham Young University Press, 1976), pp. 53-60. Monteverdi's letters are translated by Arnold and Fortune in *The Monteverdi Companion,* pp. 30-34. Even more recently Iain Fenlon has advanced the more plausible theory that the Vespers were first performed on Sunday, May 25, 1608, at "a special ceremony in Sant'Andrea in-

augurating a new order of knighthood in honour of Christ the Redeemer." This ceremony marked the beginning of the 1608 wedding festival. According to the court chronicler Follino, the ceremony was followed by a chanting of the *Te Deum,* an oration by the Bishop of Mantua, and the celebration of solemn Vespers. See Iain Fenlon, "The Monteverdi Vespers: Suggested answers to some fundamental questions," *Early Music* 5, no. 3 (July 1977): 380-387. The chief argument against Fenlon's hypothesis is the liturgical specificity of the Vespers to feasts of the Virgin and other virgin saints. See chapter V, pp. 124-125. Whether or not the wedding festivities would have justified celebration of Vespers of the Virgin is unknown. I do not agree with Fenlon's assumption that Monteverdi's Vespers would have had to have been performed in their entirety. See the Introduction, pp. 3-4, and chapter V, p. 131.

10. See De' Paoli, *Lettere,* p. 50; and De' Paoli, *Claudio Monteverdi,* p. 160.

11. Casola's letter distinguishes clearly between Monteverdi's intention to have the Mass and Vespers published and his plan to go to Rome to dedicate them to the Pope. It is only Francesco who connects the publication of the collection with the journey to Rome.

12. De' Paoli, *Lettere,* p. 50.

13. Vogel, "Claudio Monteverdi," p. 356.

14. De' Paoli, *Lettere,* pp. 50-52.

15. Malipiero, *Claudio Monteverdi,* pp. 147-149.

16. Hans Redlich, ed., *Missa "In Illo Tempore" a 6 by Claudio Monteverdi* (London: Ernst Eulenburg, 1962), p. IV. De' Paoli seems at one time to have held a similar view; see De' Paoli, *Claudio Monteverdi,* pp. 160-162.

17. Henri Prunières, *Monteverdi: His Life and Work,* trans. Marie D. Mackie (New York: E. P. Dutton & Company, 1926; reprint edition New York: Dover Publications, Inc., 1972), p. 214, note 123.

18. De' Paoli, *Lettere,* pp. 95-97.

19. See ibid., p. 50; and Denis Arnold, *Monteverdi,* revised edition (London: J. M. Dent & Sons Ltd., 1975), p. 24.

20. The appropriateness of the Mass and Vespers to Rome and Venice respectively may account for the much-noted difference in the size of the lettering of the two items on the title page. The larger print for the Mass corresponds with the naming of the dedicatee on the title page itself. Pope Paul would very likely have had little interest in music for Vespers, whose title is given a decidedly secondary place.

21. See William J. Bouwsma, *Venice and the Defense of Republican Liberty* (Berkeley: University of California Press, 1968), especially pp. 339-555.

22. Printed in De' Paoli, *Lettere,* pp. 410-411. I am grateful to Prof. Kristine Wallace for the following translation: "When I wished to send forth into the light certain ecclesiastical pieces in musical modes to be sung in chorus, I had decided to dedicate [them] to your Majesty, Pontiff of Pontiffs, than which truly none in the world of mortals approaches nearer to God, but because I recognized that to the greatest and highest, things very mean and small were not

politely dedicated, plainly I would have changed my plan if it had not finally come into my mind that material concerning divine matters by a certain right of its own demands that the title page of the work be inscribed, or rather imprinted, with the name of him who has the keys to Heaven in his hands and holds the helm of empire on earth. Therefore that the sacred harmonies, illuminated by your extraordinary and almost divine glory, may be resplendent and that by [your] supreme blessing being given, the humble hill of my talent may daily grow more and more green, and that the mouths of those speaking unfair things against Claudio may be closed, having thrown myself at your most holy feet, I offer and present these my nocturnal labors, of whatever sort they are. Wherefore, again and again I beg that you may deign with kindly countenance and cheerful mind to accept what I humbly offer, for thus it will happen that with more lively mind after this and with greater labor than before I shall be able to serve both God and the Blessed Virgin and you; farewell and live long, happy.''

23. *"& claudantur ora in Claudium loquentium iniqua."*

24. See note 7 above.

25. De' Paoli, *Lettere,* p. 374.

26. For a detailed discussion of cautionary signs see Don Harrán, "New Evidence for Musica Ficta: The Cautionary Sign," *Journal of the American Musicological Society* **29** (Spring 1976): 77-98; see also "Comments and Issues," *Journal of the American Musicological Society* **31** (Summer 1978): 385-395.

27. The significance of the *chiavette* with regard to transposition will be discussed below.

28. In the copy of the *Tenor* part-book at the University Library in Wroclaw, Poland, the part is emended to agree with the version in the *Bassus Generalis.*

29. The Wroclaw copy of the *Cantus* part-book is emended to agree with the *Bassus Generalis.*

30. The errors are actually assumed to be in the *Quintus* of the first choir, which is printed in the *Altus* part-book, and the *Tenor* of the second choir, which is notated in the *Sextus* part-book.

31. Subsequent to my having made this correction in my own transcription of *Nisi Dominus,* an examination of a microfilm copy of the part-books at the University Library at Wroclaw revealed that the semibreve *c* in the *Quintus* of the first choir had been erased, resulting in the same closing for the psalm suggested here.

32. The solution in example 9, given in several editions, assumes that the *Bassus Generalis* is a *basso seguente,* merely doubling the lowest part at any given time. However, the *partitura* in both the Mass and Vespers departs from the *seguente* principle with some frequency.

33. The position of the added rest as shown in example 12 is found in the editions by Denis Stevens, *Claudio Monteverdi: Vespers* (London: Novello and Company, Ltd., 1961), p. 55; and Gottfried Wolters, *Claudio Monteverdi: Vesperae Beatae Mariae Virginis* (Wolfenbüttel: Möseler Verlag, 1966), p. 75.

34. Stevens, *Claudio Monteverdi: Vespers,* p. 55. Used with permission. Stevens's edition omits the motets, *Sonata sopra Sancta Maria,* and *Magnificat à 6.*

35. The *Tenor* part-book at Wroclaw contains a handwritten correction identical to the one in example 15.

36. This discussion will treat general aspects of the relationship between the *Bassus Generalis* and performance practice and will not attempt a detailed catalogue of performance suggestions. The latter will appear in my edition of the Mass and Vespers to be published by the *Fondazione "Claudio Monteverdi"* of Cremona. Literature on the subject of seventeenth-century performance practice is vast and is most easily located through Mary Vinquist and Neal Zaslaw, eds., *Performance Practice: A Bibliography* (New York: W. W. Norton & Company, Inc., 1971). A discussion of performance practice in the Mass and Vespers, with views somewhat different from mine, can be found in Andreas Holschneider, "Zur Aufführungspraxis der Marien-Vesper von Monteverdi," *Hamburger Jahrbuch für Musikwissenschaft* (Hamburg: Karl Dieter Wagner, 1974), vol. I, pp. 59-68. See also Jürgen Jürgens, "Urtext und Aufführungspraxis bei Monteverdis *Orfeo* und *Marien-Vesper*" in *Claudio Monteverdi e il suo Tempo, Atti del Congresso internazionale di Studi monteverdiani, May 3-May 7, 1968*, ed. Raffaello Monterosso (Verona: La Stamperia Valdonega, 1969), pp. 269-304. A recent article on organ scores in early Baroque music prints, which appeared after this chapter was completed, generally concurs with the conclusions drawn here. See Imogene Horsley, "Full and Short Scores in the Accompaniment of Italian Church Music in the Early Baroque," *Journal of the American Musicological Society* **30**, no. 3 (Fall 1977): 466-499.

37. Evidence on the use of harpsichords is sketchy. At San Petronio in Bologna they seem to have served mainly as substitutes when organs were in disrepair. See Anne Schnoebelen, "The Concerted Mass at San Petronio in Bologna: ca. 1660-1730. A Documentary and Analytical Study" (Ph.D. dissertation, University of Illinois, 1966), pp. 327-328. Harpsichords also appeared at Santa Maria Maggiore in Bergamo well before the turn of the seventeenth century. See Jerome Roche, "Music at S. Maria Maggiore, Bergamo, 1614-1643," *Music and Letters* **47**, no. 4 (October 1966): 297. According to information discovered and communicated to me by Stephen Bonta, it was the practice at Santa Maria Maggiore to use harpsichords during Holy Week services.   .

38. A detailed eyewitness account of a performance of Mass and Vespers at the Scuola San Rocco in Venice in 1608 cites theorbos among the continuo instruments. See Stephen Bonta, "Liturgical Problems in Monteverdi's Marian Vespers," *Journal of the American Musicological Society* **20** (Spring 1967): 97-98.

39. A recording of the Vespers by the Monteverdi-Chor Hamburg and Concentus Musicus Wien under the direction of Jürgen Jürgens (Telefunken, *Das Alte Werk* SAWT 9501/02) changes continuo instruments regularly in these psalms. The propriety of the extensive use of harpsichord in this recording is questionable.

40. The bass line is mostly, but not exclusively, a *basso seguente*.

41. See Otto Kinkeldey, *Orgel und Klavier in der Musik des 16. Jahrhunderts* (Leipzig, 1910; reprint edition Hildesheim: Georg Olms, 1968), pp. 197 and 201.

42. Ibid., pp. 195-215.

43. See Carol MacClintock, *Giaches de Wert: Life and Works* (American Institute of Musicology, 1966), p. 223. The 1613 collection *Apparato Musicale* by Amante Franzoni, *maestro di cappella* at Santa Barbara at that time, contains instrumental music for use in the mass.

44. In the *Seicento* the use of boy sopranos would probably have required several singers for the part to be heard above the Sonata. In modern performances a single female soprano suffices and is very effective. There is a possibility—remote in the absence of specific instructions—that the bass line in the *Cantus* part-book was also to serve for a separate continuo instrument, to play only while the *Cantus* was singing. This would make sense only if a solo soprano or small number of boys were positioned at some distance from the main organ.

45. The relationship between these motets and contemporary sacred monody and few-voiced motets is treated in chapter V, pp. 150-156.

46. See F. T. Arnold, *The Art of Accompaniment from a Thorough-Bass* (London: Oxford University Press, 1931; reprint edition New York: Dover Publications, Inc., 1965), pp. 52 and 70. Agostino Agazzari is one of those opposed to doubling the soprano. Giovanni Paolo Cima comments on the purpose of the voice part in the *partitura* of his *Concerti ecclesiastici* of 1610 "*Et benche nel Partito in molti luoghi ci siano le gratie, come stanno nelle parti, l'ho fatto acciò si vegga lo stile; oltreche anco è di molto agiuto al cantore suonargli talvolta l'ornamento. Ma per lo più giudicarei essere bene, toccare solo il fermo. . . .*" Quoted in Luigi Ferdinando Tagliavini, "Registrazioni organistiche nei Magnificat dei 'Vespri' monteverdiani," *Rivista italiana di musicologia* 2, no. 2 (1967): 366-367.

47. These registrations are discussed in Tagliavini, "Registrazioni organistiche," pp. 365-371.

48. In the *Et exultavit, Quia fecit,* and *Suscepit Israel* of the *Magnificat à 7* and the *Et misericordia* of the *Magnificat à 6*.

49. The most extensive contemporary description of foundation and improvising instruments is Agostino Agazzari's *Del sonare sopra'l Basso con tutti li Stromenti e dell'uso loro nel Conserto* (Siena, 1607). English translation in Strunk, *Source Readings,* pp. 424-431. Agazzari's treatise has been correlated with other seventeenth-century sources in Gloria Rose, "Agazzari and the Improvising Orchestra," *Journal of the American Musicological Society* 18 (Fall 1965): 382-393.

50. See the preface to Caccini's *Le Nuove Musiche* of 1602. English translation in Strunk, *Source Readings,* pp. 377-392 and in H. Wiley Hitchcock, *Giulio Caccini: Le Nuove Musiche* (Madison: A-R Editions, Inc., 1970), pp. 43-56.

51. Telefunken SAWT 9501/02. See note 39 above.

52. Gloria Rose suggests that because Agazzari's treatise was reprinted in a collection of his motets in 1608, its description of foundation and improvising instruments would pertain to those motets. This may be true, but Giulio Cesare Monteverdi's famous *Dichiaratione* on the *prima pratica* and *seconda pratica* was printed in the *Scherzi Musicali* of 1607, to which it is largely irrelevant. Agazzari may simply have found his forthcoming motet collection of 1608 a convenient means of propagating his treatise. See Gloria Rose, "Agazzari and the Improvising Orchestra," p. 382. In my opinion the voices in all four of Monteverdi's motets are best left undoubled.

53. Note the similarity to the rubric *à 8. voci sole nel Organo* for the psalm *Laudate pueri*. Both rubrics may have the dual meaning of solo voices without instrumental doubling.

54. See Gloria Rose, "Agazzari and the Improvising Orchestra."

55. A survey of ornamentation treatises is found in Max Kuhn, *Die Verzierungs-Kunst in der Gesangs-Musik des 16.-17. Jahrhunderts* (Leipzig: Breitkopf and Härtel, 1902). See also Ernest T. Ferand, *Improvisation in Nine Centuries of Western Music,* vol. 12 of *Anthology of Music* (Cologne: Arno Volk Verlag, 1961); and Howard Mayer Brown, *Embellishing Sixteenth-Century Music* (London: Oxford University Press, 1976).

56. See, for example, Caccini's preface cited in note 50. Caccini was only one of many who expressed their opinions on tasteless virtuosi.

57. The *chiavette* in Amadino's print are the treble G clef, C_2 and C_3 clefs, and the F_3 clef.

58. The most comprehensive treatment of pitch and *chiavette* is in Arthur Mendel, "Pitch in the 16th and Early 17th Centuries," *The Musical Quarterly* **34** (1948): 28-45, 199-221, 336-357, and 575-593. A somewhat different view from Mendel's is presented in Siegfried Hermelink, "Zur Chiavettenfrage," *Bericht über den Musikwissenschaftlichen Kongress Wien, Mozartjahr 1956,* ed. Erich Schenk (Cologne: Verlag Hermann Böhlaus Nachf., 1958), pp. 264-271. See also Caroline Anne Miller, "Chiavette: A New Approach" (Master's thesis, University of California at Berkeley, 1960).

59. Mendel, "Pitch," pp. 336-357.

60. *Nigra sum, Laudate pueri, Pulchra es,* and *Sonata sopra Sancta Maria.* Giambattista Martini prints the first *Agnus Dei* of the Mass as an example for young composers of *Musica Ecclesiastica.* Martini's version, like Tonelli's *partitura,* is notated in *chiavi naturali* and transposed a fourth downward to the key of G. See Giambattista Martini, *Esemplare o sia Saggio fondamentale pratico di Contrappunto fugato, Parte seconda* (Bologna: Lelio dalla Volpe Impressore dell'Instituto delle Scienze, 1776), pp. 242-250.

61. The void notes indicate the primary tessituras. The solid note heads indicate the extreme high and low notes, encountered less frequently.

62. Mendel, "Pitch," pp. 199-221. See especially p. 206 and Table II on p. 221. From Mendel's discussion of Praetorius, it seems most likely that the pitch in use in northern Italy was approximately a half-step higher than modern pitch, which means that a notated pitch of the seventeenth century should sound higher today. Tonelli's *partitura,* therefore, would have sounded, at modern fixed pitch, approximately in A-flat instead of its notated G, and the lowest note in the bass would have approximated our E-flat. However, the fluctuation in pitch from one organ to another could have increased significantly the difference between Tonelli's notation and modern pitch.

63. Giovanni Gabrieli remarked on the scarcity of good male altos in Venice. See Denis Arnold, *Giovanni Gabrieli* (London: Oxford University Press, 1974), p. 58. The Venetian composer Giovanni Francesco Capello often avoided the alto voice altogether in his works.

64. The compasses of early seventeenth-century instruments are outlined by Praetorius in *Syntagma Musicum, Tomus Secundus, De Organographia* (Wolffenbüttel, 1618). A modern transcription is found in *Publikationen Älterer Praktischer und Theoretischer Musikwerke* (Reprint edition New York: Broude Brothers, 1966), vol. XIII, pp. 22-33. Praetorius's ranges are also reported in Sibyl Marcuse, *A Survey of Musical Instruments* (New York: Harper & Row, 1975).

CHAPTER II

A CRITICAL COMMENTARY ON THE *MISSA IN ILLO TEMPORE*

Monteverdi's *Missa In illo tempore* has received mixed reviews over the years from the composer's major biographers.[1] Published by Ricciardo Amadino together with the *Vespro della Beata Vergine* in 1610 and also surviving in a separate manuscript copy in the Vatican, this work was Monteverdi's first large-scale essay in the imitative polyphonic style of the sixteenth century.[2] It has been generally assumed that the Mass was written in order to demonstrate the composer's capacity in the *prima pratica* to both his critics and prospective employers.[3] That Monteverdi still smarted from the attacks of Artusi seems evident from the reference in the dedication to "those speaking unfair things against Claudio."[4] Monteverdi also alludes in this dedication to his "nocturnal labors,"[5] and a much-quoted letter from the Mantuan singer Bassano Casola emphasizes the effort which the Mass cost the composer.[6]

Although an analysis of the *Missa In illo tempore* proves that Monteverdi impressively surmounted the technical difficulties of treating given motives in continuous imitation, it is also apparent that he did not in this initial effort attain mastery of the polyphonic style on the level of Lassus, Palestrina, or Victoria. While Monteverdi's work is a *tour de force* in the manipulation of motives in multiple combinations, augmentation, diminution, inversion, retrogression, and paraphrase, the composer's concentration on all-pervasive imitation yields a density of texture that is rarely relieved. In only two sections, the *Et incarnatus* and the *Benedictus,* does Monteverdi accede to a homophonic style.[7] A reduced number of voices appears only in the *Crucifixus,* where the *Quintus* (second tenor) and *Bassus* are *tacet.*[8] Nowhere do we find the constantly fluctuating textures and combinations of parts that contribute so importantly to the variety and vitality of the six-voice masses of the late Renaissance masters. Monteverdi is so severe in his unremitting imitation investing all parts that the *Missa In illo tempore* may be considered more reactionary than conservative.[9] Strict, pervasive imitation was not characteristic of the larger masses of the late *Cinquecento,* but rather of the four and five-part masses of the first half of the century. In composing for six voices Monteverdi exhibited the modern interest in larger and thicker sonorities, but he did not seem to realize the necessity for variety of texture and the juxtaposition of smaller and larger voice groupings in the handling of so many parts.[10] In his intense desire to master polyphonic imitation, he ignored other vital aspects of mass composition that were common currency among those who practiced the polyphonic art regularly. Monteverdi may have overcome Artusi's objections to his voice leading and dissonance treatment through the development of an awesome imitative technique, but there was more than that to the *stile antico* of the late Renaissance.

Additional problems arise from insufficient tonal variety in the work. The most modern feature of the Mass is Monteverdi's fully tonal orientation, but his overwhelmingly predominant C major proves tiresome in the end.[11] The close imitation between the two sopranos (*Cantus* and *Sextus*) results in repetitious emphasis on certain pitches, especially *g* ", to the point where they eventually grate on the ears.[12] Monteverdi also fails to vary his harmony sufficiently, as illustrated by passages where the bass continually moves back and forth between tonic and dominant in the modern sense (see example 1). It is not that Monteverdi was incapable of coping successfully with harmonic and tonal limitations; in the accompanying Vespers he did so with remarkable virtuosity. But in the Vespers he felt free to vary textures and styles, to manipulate widely divergent rhythms, to experiment with differing sonorities. In the Mass everything is tightly constrained with an often stultifying rigidity. In striving so strenuously to prove his contrapuntal technique, Monteverdi denied himself the variety and flexibility necessary to make that technique truly effective.

Monteverdi's unusual parody procedure in the Mass is both a source and a symptom of his difficulties. Rather than following the more common method of using a pre-existing composition as a structural framework upon which to expand, he has chosen instead to extract motives from his model to be recombined in a wholly new contrapuntal fabric.[13] His selection of the motet *In illo tempore* by Gombert is indicative of the reactionary outlook of the work.[14] Gombert, who died about 1556, represents in his mastery of imitation a continuation of the Josquin tradition. In extending this mastery to works for five and six voices, while simultaneously abandoning Josquin's characteristic voice pairing, Gombert creates some of the most dense textures of the first half of the sixteenth century.

Gombert's motet *In illo tempore* had two important advantages for Monteverdi: it contained motives with a strong harmonic basis, and it was fully Ionian, with no trace of the older Church modes. The work was therefore quite suitable to Monteverdi's own tonal inclinations. Like the Mass, the motet is for six voices (although only five normally sound at any given time), and it has little harmonic and tonal variety. But because of its short

EXAMPLE 1. *Sanctus*

duration, these factors are not shortcomings. It is only with Monteverdi's enormous temporal extension of these features without adequate consideration for the resulting aesthetic effect that difficulties arise. Ironically, although Gombert's motet is continuously polyphonic, it is actually much less rigorously imitative than Monteverdi's Mass.[15]

Monteverdi's desire to advertise his newly-won technique was so strong that in both the Vatican manuscript copy and Amadino's print he prefaced the Mass with a table of motives, or *fughe,* extracted from the motet.[16] Hans Redlich has located these motives in the motet, where they occasionally differ from Monteverdi's *fughe* in rhythm and even in pitch.[17] Monteverdi uses all of the main motives of Gombert's work, though not in the same sequence. Only Gombert's opening subject occupies a comparable role in the Mass, serving as the head motive for several sections. Nor does Monteverdi employ the ten *fughe* in the order they appear in either of his own tables. Only the *Fuga prima* is located in both tables in a position equivalent to its significance in the Mass.

Monteverdi's manipulation of Gombert's motives and his command of imitative techniques constitute the most impressive and positive features of his Mass. An analysis of these elements not only yields an appreciation of Monteverdi's technical accomplishments, but also confirms the *"studio et fatica grande"* described by Bassano Casola.[18]

The opening *Kyrie* offers only hints of the sophistication to come. It is based almost entirely on *Fuga* 1, which at the outset is imitated at the close time interval of a semibreve. However, Monteverdi frequently varies the temporal interval of imitation throughout the section. The subject also appears several times in augmentation, with even the augmented versions treated imitatively. These augmentations create the impression of a long-note *cantus firmus* during much of *Kyrie I,* and Monteverdi returns often to similar augmentations throughout the Mass for the same *cantus firmus* effect. It should be noted that *cantus firmi* in both long and short note values are the structural foundation of the majority of the pieces in the Vespers, so the technique is common to both highly divergent parts of the 1610 collection.

Already in the opening *Kyrie* of the Mass the main imitative subject is joined by a countersubject, consisting of descending scales of varying lengths. While the augmented form of *Fuga* 1 is presented in two of the voices, the others engage in sequences derived from the downward scale (see example 2). These descending sequences become an essential part of the contrapuntal fabric of the Mass, particularly in approaching major cadences.

The *Christe* is based exclusively on *Fuga* 4, and at the very beginning this motive is combined with its own inversion after a lapse of only a minim. The order of the two entries of the motive is then immediately reversed in

EXAMPLE 2. *Kyrie I*

EXAMPLE 3. *Christe*

EXAMPLE 4a. *Christe*

EXAMPLE 4a continued.

EXAMPLE 4b. *Dixit Dominus*

another pair of voices (see example 3). Throughout the *Christe* the inverted form is more prominent than the original subject, testifying to Monteverdi's willingness to manipulate Gombert's *fughe* rather than adhere strictly to their original shapes. After the initial imitative passage, sequences derived from the first three notes of the inverted motive govern the entire texture. These sequences outline a descending diatonic scale and are closely related to sequences from *Dixit Dominus* in the Vespers (see examples 4a and 4b).[19] The falling sequences occur in various rhythmic forms in different voices, but all are based in one way or another on a descending scale.

Kyrie II uses these sequences as its main substance. Here Monteverdi employs a slightly varied form of *Fuga 2*, which possesses its own internal sequence of descending broken thirds. But he soon abandons the complete *fuga* altogether in order to extend the broken thirds to ever-increasing lengths. The descending thirds are themselves a simple elaboration of a scale and are therefore easily combined with other scale-derived sequential motives (see example 5). In the immediately ensuing measures Monteverdi engages in invertible counterpoint through the interchange of various parts (see example 6).

In the opening movement of the Mass, Monteverdi has already demonstrated imitation at varying time intervals, augmentation, inversion, and the free interchange of different contrapuntal lines. In addition, he has displayed a flexible approach to the motives themselves, freely altering their rhythms and even their pitch configurations. In both the *Christe* and *Kyrie II* he virtually abandons the *fughe* in favor of lengthy sequences whose relationship to Gombert's motives is sometimes rather tenuous. The significance of these sequences in the construction of the Mass as a whole cannot be overemphasized, and the reappearance of similar patterns in *Dixit Dominus* and many other polyphonic sections of the Vespers illustrates how much elaborations on the descending scalar sequence dominated Monteverdi's contrapuntal thinking at this time.[20]

The monothematic character of each section of the *Kyrie* necessarily gives way to greater thematic diversity in the much longer *Gloria* and *Credo*. The *Gloria*, divided in the traditional manner into two large sections, eventually uses all ten of the *fughe*. Monteverdi's normal procedure is to employ one *fuga* at a time, contrapuntally dovetailing each monothematic passage with the next, each new passage being based on a new *fuga*. Except for the opening *Fuga 1*, the order of presentation of the motives is unrelated to either of Monteverdi's tables. As in *Kyrie II*, *Fuga 2* easily leads to descending sequences of broken thirds which form a new motive in their own right. Monteverdi sometimes employs brief countersubjects that are not traceable to any of the ten *fughe*.

Inverted forms of motives also appear on occasion, as do retrograde, embellished, and paraphrased versions (see examples 7a and 7b). Lengthy

EXAMPLE 5. *Kyrie II*

EXAMPLE 6. *Kyrie II*

EXAMPLE 7a. *Gloria*

EXAMPLE 7b. *Gloria*

motives, such as *Fuga* 3, are at times truncated rather than continued to completion. As in all sections of the *Kyrie,* both segments of the *Gloria* conclude with sequences derived from descending scales. While Gombert also uses descending scalar fifths near the end of his motet, they are not arranged in sequences and function primarily as embellishments, increasing the rhythmic activity. Monteverdi's scalar sequences, by contrast, generate a strong harmonic impetus toward the final cadence. It is this quest for a modern cadential harmonic drive that engenders these sequences in the first place, and they consequently assume a paradoxical and anachronistic role in the otherwise archaic texture.

There are brief passages in the *Gloria* where Monteverdi for the first time unites more than one of Gombert's motives in counterpoint. In the *Qui tollis* section, which opens with a retrograde of *Fuga* 1, the original form of this motive is quickly added and then the retrograde dovetails with a variant of *Fuga* 8. The derivation of the variant from *Fuga* 8 is made explicit only by that subject's appearance in "pure" form in the *Bassus* at the word *miserere* (see example 8).[21] Similar combinations of motives occur elsewhere in the *Qui tollis,* especially at *Quoniam tu solus Sanctus,* but they are otherwise uncommon through most of the *Gloria.* The overall structure of the *Gloria* is rounded, for the movement closes as it opened, with the original form of *Fuga* 1.

The diverse treatments of the *fughe* in the *Gloria* serve as a point of departure for a much freer and more flexible manipulation of the motives in the *Credo.* This movement, which also begins with *Fuga* 1, combines two or more subjects simultaneously far more frequently. Inverted, retrograde, and paraphrased forms are common. The longer *fughe,* 1, 2, and 3, are often truncated, while short motives, such as *Fughe* 6 and 8, are at times extended. Broken thirds in descending sequences emerge even more prominently, and now Monteverdi does not even bother to demonstrate their relationship to *Fuga* 2. Paraphrases of certain motives are increasingly further removed from the original form (see example 9).[22] At *Et in Spiritum Sanctum Dominum, Fuga* 1, utilized as a long-note *cantus firmus,* is combined with scalar fifths, illustrating the origin of the scale patterns in the embellishment of the simple fifths that are common to several of the original *fughe* (see example 10). In the concluding segment of the *Credo,* beginning at *Et in Spiritum Sanctum,* paraphrases, inversions, interval expansions, truncated motives, long-note *cantus firmi,* broken thirds, descending and rising sequences (rising sequences at *Et expecto resurrectionem*), and even a freely composed countersubject all combine to create a texture of great variety and vivacity. This is one of the more successful sections of the Mass, the flexibility of the polyphony evidently liberating Monteverdi's imagination with felicitous results.

The two central sections of the *Credo,* the *Et incarnatus* and the

EXAMPLE 8. *Gloria*

EXAMPLE 9. *Credo* (continued on next page)

Crucifixus, provide the only relief in this movement from Monteverdi's consistency of tonality and texture. The *Et incarnatus*, in interpreting the mystery of the incarnation, begins abruptly with the exotic chord of E major, which serves as dominant to the tonality of A (mostly A minor). The texture of this passage is primarily chordal with slow rhythmic movement, though the homophony is enlivened by limited polyphonic activity.[23] This section in Monteverdi's Mass is particularly striking and beautiful, but because of the brevity of the text, it is unfortunately quite short, with a duration of only fourteen breves.

The following *Crucifixus* returns to imitative polyphony, but with a reduced texture of four voices.[24] A lighter and more ethereal sonority is achieved by the elimination of the *Bassus* and *Quintus*. At *Et iterum* there is a lengthy passage based exclusively on descending sequences of broken thirds, treated imitatively in all voices. In portions of this passage, the simultaneous combination of broken thirds and a descending scale confirms once again their close relationship. These broken thirds and other more complicated sequences so permeate the Mass that it often seems that Monteverdi has reverted to them whenever he has run out of ideas for dealing anew with Gombert's *fughe*. In the Vespers such sequences are em-

EXAMPLE 9 continued.

ployed more sparingly and are confined to passages where they form a fundamental element in a large structure or serve as polyphonic climaxes, but in the Mass they are less convincing, less an essential outgrowth of either the texture or the structure. While these sequences undoubtedly help unify the Mass, they are at times overly long and obvious. In contrast to the sophisticated handling of the *fughe,* especially *Fuga* 1, the sequences usually do not give an impression of artfulness or skill in contrapuntal technique. Their purpose is to create an irresistible melodic and harmonic drive in their unremitting descent and repetition, but even though they are effective at some cadences, elsewhere they can sound rather awkward and out of place, as if Monteverdi were at a loss for anything better to do.

The importance of sequences and scales in the Mass has gradually increased through the first three movements to the point where they serve as the primary material for the entire *Sanctus,* except for the *Benedictus* segment. In the *Sanctus,* sequential processes are more successful than in any other movement. The effect is particularly lovely at the very outset. The variety of ways in which Monteverdi treats the sequence hints at the magnificent use he would make of descending broken thirds in the posthumously published Mass of 1650, where this motive is expanded through diversity of texture and rhythm to encompass the entire composition.[25] Some of that

EXAMPLE 10. *Credo*

diversity also characterizes the *Sanctus* of the *Missa In illo tempore,* but Monteverdi did not in this earlier work achieve the harmonic variety of his later Mass. In the *Pleni sunt coeli* the two sopranos return over and over again to their high *g″*, eventually becoming tedious, while the bass is constrained to outlining repeatedly tonic and dominant harmonies (see example 1, page 49).

The *Benedictus,* with its opening E major chord and primarily homophonic texture, is reminiscent of the *Et incarnatus* of the *Credo*. The harmony is more varied, however, with cadences in A minor, D minor, G major, and C major. While Monteverdi's *Et incarnatus* is traditional in its homophonic style and somewhat exotic harmonies, the *Benedictus* is unusual in both these respects. In sixteenth-century masses *à 6* the *Benedictus* was very often set for a reduced number of voices in a highly imitative texture. In composing the *Benedictus* in the same style as the *Et incarnatus,* Monteverdi may be deliberately drawing a parallel between the significance of the phrase *Benedictus qui venit in nomine Domini* and the text of the *Et incarnatus,* referring to the appearance of God made man.

The music of the *Benedictus* is related to the original *fughe* only in its descending and ascending scalar patterns, which, as we have seen in the *Et in Spiritum Sanctum* of the *Credo,* are derived by filling out the skip of a fifth common to several of Gombert's motives. Also prominent in the *Benedictus* is the leap of a fourth, which is allied by inversion to the beginning of *Fuga*

EXAMPLE 11. *Sanctus*

10 (see example 11, especially the lower voices). Following traditional practice, the concluding *Osanna* repeats precisely the music of the first *Osanna*.

After departing almost entirely from Gombert's *fughe* in the *Sanctus,* Monteverdi returns to a limited selection of these motives for the *Agnus Dei.* The *Agnus* is divided into two sections, the last one expanded to seven voices by the addition of a second bass, thus concluding the Mass with a thicker texture and heavier sonority. Such augmentation by one or more voices is a frequent practice in the final *Agnus* of many sixteenth-century masses.

Rather than begin with *Fuga* 1 as a head motive, the first *Agnus* commences with an inversion of *Fuga* 4 very similar in shape to the opening of the *Christe* (see examples 12 and 3). This inversion is closely related to *Fuga* 3, and Monteverdi highlights the connection by constructing his polyphony from both original and inverted forms of the latter motive at *miserere nobis*. Once again the descending sequence appears as a primary polyphonic technique, comprising the larger part of *Agnus I.* But here the sequences are much more varied and rhythmically complex than the broken thirds dispersed elsewhere throughout the Mass. Because the patterns in *Agnus I* are never obtrusive and their disposition in the polyphonic texture constantly changes, the entire passage is quite successful. Approaching the cadence Monteverdi even injects *Fuga* 3 into the texture as a long-note *cantus firmus,* migrating successively from one voice to another.

EXAMPLE 12. *Agnus Dei*

There is a close and obvious relationship between *Agnus I* and the *Christe*, both in the motives used and in their subsequent development. The *Agnus*, which is almost twice as long, exhibits greater flexibility in the handling of sequences and increased fluidity of motion emanating from the character and variety of the rhythmic patterns. Even in *Agnus I*, though, the sequences occasionally sound forced, rather than a natural outgrowth of the polyphonic style.

Agnus II, as already remarked, concludes the Mass with an expanded texture of seven voices. *Fuga* 1, which has not been heard since near the conclusion of the *Credo,* functions as the head motive and primary material of this section. The return of *Fuga* 1 at the end of the Mass stresses its cyclic role for the entire work analogous to its office in forming a rounded structure for the *Gloria.* Once the motive has been presented, Monteverdi quickly fills out the opening leap with the intervening notes of the sacle, as he had done earlier in the *Et in Spiritum Sanctum.* These scales then move in either direction and are extended even beyond the octave. *Fuga* 1 also appears in retrograde, eventually combining with its original form and with *Fuga* 6. The triadic shape of *Fuga* 6, with its clear harmonic outline, is well suited to enhancing the cadential drive of the closing. Near both the beginning and the end of *Agnus II, Fuga* 1 emerges as a sustained *cantus firmus.* The vigorous cadential motion of *Fughe* 1 and 6, the long-note *cantus firmus,* and the thicker texture of seven voices all contribute to a forceful conclusion for the entire Mass.

Study of the *Missa In illo tempore* demonstrates that Monteverdi's "nocturnal labors" and *"studio et fatica grande"* bore fruit in his ability to manipulate Gombert's subjects with impressive skill. He has added to his workshop techniques that by 1610 had become somewhat antiquated: the weaving of a continuous polyphonic fabric with imitation at varying time intervals, the polyphonic combination of multiple subjects, the inversion, retrogression, augmentation, and paraphrase of motives, and the long-note *cantus firmus.* But technical skill does not of itself make great art, and Monteverdi did not master his new-found technique to the point where it could fully serve the aesthetic requirements of a work of such dimensions. His frequent reliance on lengthy sequences to spin out the texture is evidence of his discomfort with the polyphonic medium and his inability to work freely and uninhibitedly with it. This uneasiness and constraint are striking in contrast to the seemingly infinite imagination and virtuosity of the multi-faceted and stylistically varied Vespers. In the Vespers, Monteverdi was the complete master of every situation, and the enthusiasm with which performances are received today is further confirmation of their artistic success. Modern interest in the Mass, however, is focused chiefly on its documentary and biographical significance. As a work of art it is uneven, containing many lovely and effective passages, but lacking consistent vitality.

An inquiry into what role the *Missa In illo tempore* played in Monteverdi's compositional development, aside from the work's immediate function as proof that he could write in the *stile antico*, produces no definitive answer. Very likely his enhanced skill in the imitation and manipulation of motives served him well in the imitative duets that form so significant a part of the *concertato* style of the contemporaneous Vespers and later sacred and secular works. On the other hand, Monteverdi's two subsequent masses in the *prima pratica* show little dependence upon the *Missa In illo tempore.*[26] Both of these masses are set for only four voices, but even with fewer parts Monteverdi employs the full texture rather sparingly, concentrating much of his attention on two-voiced passages resembling his *concertato* technique. The rhythms in the masses are certainly more restrained in the use of dotted patterns than the *concertato* madrigals or *seconda pratica* sacred music, and rapid embellishments are avoided altogether. But there is a liveliness and lilt to these two masses that is missing from the more turgid and dense *Missa In illo tempore.* Monteverdi was obviously far more comfortable with the thinner texture and *concertato* treatment of the parts in these later masses, and they evince a buoyancy and natural flow that he was unable to achieve in his first effort in the genre.

The 1650 Mass is especially revealing of the differences between these later works and the *Missa In illo tempore,* since its motivic basis is the same descending sequence of broken thirds so prominent in the parody mass of 1610. But where these sequences appear somewhat unnatural in the archaic style of the earlier work, they are the essence of vitality in the later composition. In the 1650 Mass they are handled with deftness and virtuosity, begetting a fluidity, forward impetus, and motivic cohesion that constitute Monteverdi's best work in the *prima pratica* and an outstanding contribution to the mass repertoire by any standards.

It appears justifiable to conclude that in the *Missa In illo tempore* Monteverdi learned as many negative lessons as he did new technical skills. He never again attempted such systematic imitation and henceforth abjured altogether such dense textures. In the future his desire for a large sound would be satisfied by chordal sonorities, and extended imitation would be confined primarily to duets of identical voices or instruments. In these homophonic and duet textures he was able to utilize to the fullest his natural rhythmic exuberance and superb coloristic sense, both of which failed him in the 1610 Mass. The *Missa In illo tempore* was a one-time experiment, possibly prompted by Artusi's attacks, but probably also necessitated by Monteverdi's search for ecclesiastical employment. In retrospect it seems fully appropriate that he did not find a position in Rome or Milan, the bastions of conservative sacred music, but in Venice, where it was the Vespers, not the Mass, that qualified him in the eyes of the Procurators of San Marco.[27]

NOTES

1. Denis Arnold has moderate praise for some aspects of the Mass while explicitly and implicitly criticizing other features. Arnold, *Monteverdi* (London: J. M. Dent & Sons, Ltd., 1963), p. 138. See also the revised edition of 1975, p. 138. Leo Schrade has only admiration for Monteverdi's technical mastery and his "purest imitation of the sixteenth-century style." Schrade, *Monteverdi, Creator of Modern Music* (New York: W. W. Norton & Company, Inc., 1950), p. 250. Hans Redlich is non-committal, noting only the work's austerity and "remarkable contrasts in colour-effects" in the *Crucifixus.* Redlich, *Claudio Monteverdi: Life and Works,* trans. Kathleen Dale (London: Oxford University Press, 1952), p. 123. Henri Prunières, while commenting on the Mass's archaisms, is unreserved in his praise of specific passages. Prunières, *Monteverdi: His Life and Work,* trans. Marie D. Mackie (New York: E. P. Dutton & Company, 1926; reprint edition by Dover Publications, Inc., 1972), pp. 112-115. Guido Pannain feels the Mass must be taken as an important part of Monteverdi's artistic personality, not simply prompted by external practical considerations or Artusi's attacks upon the composer. Pannain stresses the work's tranquility and smoothness, "very far from Palestrinian transports." Guglielmo Barblan, Claudio Gallico, and Guido Pannain, *Claudio Mon-*

teverdi (Turin: Edizioni RAI Radiotelevisione italiana, 1967), p. 333. Domenico De' Paoli also remarks on the extreme rigor and archaism of the Mass as well as its very solid architecture: the "closed" style of the work does not impede "the beauty of certain melodic phrases" or "moments of sudden illumination." On the other hand, De' Paoli also refers to "stylistic attitudes which began to seem a little arid and scholastic." De' Paoli, *Claudio Monteverdi* (Milan: Editore Ulrico Hoepli, 1945), pp. 163-164. Denis Stevens's recent book on Monteverdi treats the Mass in only a cursory fashion and draws no critical conclusions at all. Stevens, *Monteverdi: Sacred, Secular, and Occasional Music* (Rutherford: Fairleigh Dickinson University Press, 1978), p. 68. None of Monteverdi's biographers undertakes a thoroughgoing critical study of the work and all shy away from comprehensive critical judgments. The only detailed study of the Mass is in Gerhard Hust, *Untersuchungen zu Claudio Monteverdis Messkompositionen* (Ph.D. dissertation, Ruprecht-Karl-Universität in Heidelberg, 1970), hereafter cited as Hust. Another briefer but trenchant discussion is in Jerome Roche, "Monteverdi and the *Prima Prattica*," *The Monteverdi Companion*, ed. Denis Arnold and Nigel Fortune (London: Faber and Faber, 1968), pp. 167-178. Roche cites several faults in the Mass. The earliest published analysis of a portion of the Mass, the first *Agnus Dei*, appears in Giambattista Martini, *Esemplare o sia Saggio Fondamentale Pratico di Contrappunto Fugato, Parte Seconda* (Bologna: Lelio dalla Volpe, 1776), pp. 242-250. The *Agnus* is used as a model of the contrapuntal sacred style for young composers.

2. The manuscript is *Biblioteca Apostolica Vaticana, Cappella Sistina* Ms. 107. This source is discussed in chapter I, pp. 8-15. Don Siro Cisilino of the Cini Foundation in Venice has transcribed and published an anonymous collection of three masses under the title *Claudio Monteverdi: Tre Missae* (Milan: Universal Edition, 1974). Cisilino considers these works to pertain to the period around 1600 and to be Monteverdi's answer to the criticisms of the theorist Giovanni Maria Artusi. There is no evidence to support Cisilino's attribution to Monteverdi, however, and the rationale he offers in his preface is unsound.

3. See chapter I, pp. 11-12.

4. See chapter I, pp. 13-15.

5. Ibid.

6. See chapter I, pp. 9-10.

7. Throughout the second half of the sixteenth century it was customary to begin the *Et incarnatus* with a chordal texture and longer note values than used in other parts of a mass. In this section the mystery of the incarnation was also frequently interpreted by means of unusual harmonies resulting from chromatic alterations in the prevailing mode.

8. See chapter I, pp. 28-29. Reduction of the number of parts in the *Crucifixus* was another very common sixteenth-century practice. Often one or more lower voices are *tacet*, as in most of Gombert's masses and in Monteverdi's Mass, but there are also numerous instances where upper parts drop out or the reduced texture is spread more evenly across the vocal ranges.

9. See Hust, p. 99: "Monteverdi steht in seinem thematisch transparenten Parodieverfahren dem des (ausgehenden) 15. Jahrhunderts wesentlich näher als dem—freilich schon mit Obrecht einsetzenden—Zeitaler [*sic*] der 'Parodiemesse' im engeren Sinne. Die Ausrichtung

der Komposition an einlinigen Gebilden, der Aufbau mittels 'thematischer Bausteine' ist ihm mit jenem Verfahren gemeinsam.''

10. One of Gombert's own six-voice masses, the *Missa Quam pulchra es* of 1532, also entails some very dense textures resulting from the thoroughly polyphonic treatment of all parts. Imitation is especially strict in this work, which conceivably could have served as a model for Monteverdi's own imitative techniques. See Joseph Schmidt-Görg, ed., *Nicolai Gombert: Opera Omnia* (American Institute of Musicology, 1963), vol. III, pp. 1-52.

11. C major is itself only a notational convention and represents neither an absolute pitch nor the key in which the Mass would actually have been sung. See the discussion of pitch and transposition in chapter I, pp. 37-40. Only two sections of the Mass, the *Et incarnatus* and *Benedictus*, provide any real contrast of key.

12. This is especially noticeable in the *Credo,* from *Et in Spiritum Sanctum* to the end, and in the first section of the *Sanctus.*

13. Monteverdi's procedure resembles Gombert's in the *Missa Quam pulchra es* cited in note 10. See the Foreword to Schmidt-Görg, *Nicolai Gombert*, vol. III.

14. The Marian text of Gombert's motet makes it a suitable source for a mass dedicated to the Virgin.

15. See Hust, pp. 84-85.

16. The numbering of the *fughe* is somewhat different between the two sources. See chapter I, p. 13. In the analysis below, the numbering of the motives is based on Amadino's print.

17. Hans F. Redlich, ed., *Missa "In Illo Tempore" a 6 by Claudio Monteverdi* (London: Ernst Eulenburg, 1962), pp. VIII-IX.

18. See chapter I, pp. 9-10.

19. See Roche, "Monteverdi and the *Prima Prattica,"* p. 178, where other resemblances between the Mass and the Vespers are described.

20. See Hust, pp. 73-78. Sequences of the type described here are not confined solely to Monteverdi's 1610 print. His posthumous four-voice mass, first published in 1650, is based throughout on some of the same sequential patterns. See the discussion below and the analysis of the latter work in Reginald Smith Brindle, "Monteverdi's G minor Mass: an Experiment in Construction," *Musical Quarterly* 54, no. 3 (July 1968): 352-360.

21. See Hust, pp. 64-65.

22. Hust sees the *Cantus* part as deriving from the inversion of *Fuga* 1. Ibid., p. 64.

23. See note 7 above.

24. See chapter I, pp. 28-29, note 8 above, and example 9.

25. See Brindle, "Monteverdi's G minor Mass."

26. These two masses were published in the *Selva Morale e Spirituale* of 1640 and the posthumous collection of 1650 (1651), *Messa a Quattro Voci et Salmi*. Aside from Malipiero's *Tutte le Opere di Claudio Monteverdi*, easily accessible modern editions are by Denis Arnold, *Messa a 4 voci da cappella by Claudio Monteverdi (1641)* (London: Ernst Eulenburg, Ltd., 1962); and Hans F. Redlich, *Messa a 4 Voci da cappella by Claudio Monteverdi (1651)* (London: Ernst Eulenburg, Ltd., 1952).

27. See chapter I, pp. 10-12. Denis Arnold has discovered evidence that Monteverdi underwent a public *prova* in Venice prior to his appointment, the music of which must have been drawn from the 1610 Vespers. See Arnold, "The Monteverdian Succession at St. Mark's," *Music and Letters* 42, no. 3 (July 1961): 205-211.

CHAPTER III

PARODY AND VARIATION IN MONTEVERDI'S VESPERS

From late 1606 through the summer of 1610 Monteverdi was immersed in a series of compositional projects that were to prove of immense importance to the history of Western music. Under great pressure and in the midst of terrible personal crises,[1] he completed four major works, all of them employing stylistic and technical features with which he had had virtually no previous experience. Two of these projects were operatic: L'Orfeo, which was first performed in late February 1607, and Arianna, premiered on May 28, 1608.[2] The other two consisted of sacred music, published as the Mass and Vespers of the Blessed Virgin, dated the calends of September, 1610.[3] Of these latter two works we have no certain information concerning performances in Mantua.[4]

In all four of these extraordinarily large efforts Monteverdi was faced with completely new compositional problems. Aside from the recently invented dramatic recitative, L'Orfeo raised unprecedented questions of structural organization. Before L'Orfeo, Monteverdi's published repertoire had consisted exclusively of short madrigals and youthful Sacrae Cantiunculae, none of which demanded structural planning on a large scale.[5] But the new music drama did require such organization, and among the many remarkable aspects of L'Orfeo is a multiplicity of ingenious solutions to the formal problems of both single numbers and entire acts. In individual pieces Monteverdi's structures are for the most part based upon strophic variations. On larger organizational levels we find symmetrical arrangements of personae, scenes, and musical settings.

Although Monteverdi's subsequent opera, Arianna, is lost except for the famous Lamento, it is probable that the organizational means were similar to L'Orfeo, especially in view of the haste in which the composer was forced to work.[6]

The Missa In illo tempore of 1610 presented Monteverdi with quite different problems pertaining to traditional imitative techniques and the style of Netherlandish polyphony, another area in which he was inexperienced.[7] But even if Monteverdi found the polyphonic style difficult, he could never-theless rely upon a universal and long-established tradition for his models. In the Vespers, printed together with the Mass, the case was just the oppo-site, since there were no precedents for either the stylistic diversity of the collection as a whole or the construction and organization of *concertato* sacred compositions of such large dimensions.[8]

In his two operas of 1607 and 1608, Monteverdi had the advantage of a dramatic plot as well as elaborate staging and costuming to help capture his audience. But with the lengthy Vespers, the series of liturgical and inter-polated texts bore no such benefits. What is more, the great diversity of musical styles in this collection and the expansion of most of the individual pieces well beyond conventional lengths could have threatened the artistic integrity and cohesion of the entire Vesper service.[9] Indeed, finding a means for constructing and holding together such a huge body of divergent material was a compositional challenge of staggering proportions.

Monteverdi uses many different points of departure for the music of his Vespers,[10] but the organizing force underlying nearly all of the fourteen pieces is the process of variation, expanded and deepened far beyond anything found in *L'Orfeo*. As in the opera, symmetrical arrangements of the various sections are evident in three of the larger works.[11] In addition, two of the pieces are parody compositions in which the parody process often borders closely on the techniques of variation.

Those portions of the Vespers involving parody, unlike the *Missa In illo tempore,* are wholly dependent on Monteverdi's own compositions. The opening respond, *Domine ad adiuvandum,* has long been recognized as an elaboration and expansion of the toccata introducing *L'Orfeo.* Less well known is that one of the two *Magnificats* is a parody of the other. In the re-spond, the *Orfeo* toccata is lengthened and enlarged by several means: its simple motives are expanded through additional repetition, a six-voice choir (SSATTB) chanting in measured *falsobordone* is superimposed on the or-chestra,[12] triple-meter *ritornelli* are inserted between the verses of the text, and an *Alleluia* based on the *ritornelli* and combining voices and in-struments is appended as a new conclusion. Another significant, though easily overlooked, alteration is the addition of a second treble part for *cor-netto* and violin in the instrumental ensemble. This second part generates an imitative duet with the already existing first part and thereby brings the re-spond into correspondence with the numerous sections throughout the Vespers in which two voices or instruments in the same register are paired in imitation. These duets are one of the most consistent features of the Vespers and make an important contribution to the collection's musical cohesion. The augmentation of the texture in *Domine ad adiuvandum* by this second treble part suggests a purposeful attempt by Monteverdi to unify the re-spond with other pieces in the print.

General similarities have also been noted in the past between the two *Magnificat*s in the Vespers, one *à 6* with organ accompaniment and the other *à 7* with six additional *obbligato* instruments.[13] Each of the two *Magnificat*s is subdivided into twelve sections corresponding with the verses of the text and the Doxology. Of these twelve segments, ten have some form of identity between the two settings. It is not possible to determine with certainty which *Magnificat* is a parody of which, but the musical analysis that follows strongly suggests that the smaller six-voice setting served as the basis for the larger one with instruments.

The nature of the parallels between the two canticles differs from one section to the next. The treatment of the opening word, *Magnificat*, is very similar in both settings. The basses of both versions have identical pitches; only the rhythm differs slightly. The polyphonic texture of the *Magnificat à 6* increases in two-bar phrases: first a single voice, then four voices, and finally all six. But the texture of the seven-voice setting is built from groups of one, three, and seven parts with overlapping rather than separate phrases.

EXAMPLE 1a. *Magnificat à 6, Anima mea*

EXAMPLE 1b. *Magnificat à 7, Anima mea*

The continuation of the opening verse with *anima mea Dominum* likewise proceeds in parallel settings (see examples 1a and 1b). The *Magnificat à 7* has a reduced vocal texture with one voice rather than two, so the passage is only half as long. There are also some important differences in the bass lines. Where the bass unfolds in a somewhat amorphous scalar form in the setting *à 6* (example 1a), it is tightened into more discrete motivic units in the other *Magnificat,* causing alterations in the details of the harmony (example 1b).

A different kind of relationship obtains between the two settings of the *Et exultavit*. Both versions consist of a virtuoso tenor duet with a Magnificat-tone *cantus firmus* in the alto and organ continuo (see examples 2a and 2b). Even though the *Magnificat à 6* is in triple meter and the *Magnificat à 7* in duple time, the basses have nearly identical pitches through *in Deo*. But after that point the larger *Magnificat* deviates from the momentary D minor toward F major and an eventual conclusion on the tonic G minor, while the smaller *Magnificat* continues and ends in D minor with only a brief hint at F major shortly before the final cadence.

The tenor parts of the two settings diverge more gradually than the bass lines. The two tenors begin quite similarly, though the melisma of the *Magnificat à 6* expands to cover a wider range. The sequential repetition beginning at the second *et exultavit* follows the same pattern in both pieces, but the conclusion of the phrase with *spiritus meus* is different. In the *Magnificat à 7* the text is repeated and there is more complex rhythmic interaction between the voices. After the cadence the vocal parts diverge significantly, even though the harmony remains the same in both canticles. The large *Magnificat* treats the words *in Deo* with shorter melismatic patterns, which imitate one another at briefer time intervals. These melismatic figures no longer have much in common with those of the *Magnificat à 6*. As described above, the harmony changes in the midst of this passage, and *salutari meo* receives more extended and more complex melismatic treatment in the *Magnificat à 7*. Thus the similar openings of the two pieces gradually give way to greater and greater divergence until only the general character of both settings remains the same at the end.

A still different type of relationship emerges in the next section. Both *Magnificat*s present the verse *Quia respexit* in plainchant in the tenor, but the *obbligato* instrumental forces of the *Magnificat à 7* engender an obvious distinction between the two versions. Nevertheless, both are constructed on the same pattern, consisting of an introductory *ritornello* in triple meter followed by the plainchant verse in duple time and completed by the return of the *ritornello*, which accompanies the concluding words, *omnes generationes*. The organ *ritornello* of the *Magnificat à 6* shares little with the instrumental *ritornello* of the other setting aside from its structural position, meter, and generally scalar bass; the two *ritornelli* even begin in different

EXAMPLE 2a. *Magnificat à 6, Et exultavit* (cont. on next page)

EXAMPLE 2a continued.

EXAMPLE 2b. *Magnificat à 7, Et exultavit* (cont. on next page)

EXAMPLE 2b continued.

keys. During the verse, however, where the two settings have the same chant, there are both similarities and significant differences in the bass lines. At first the basses are identical, but the subsequent successive entrances of paired *pifare*, trombones, and flutes in the *Magnificat à 7*, which result in a sizable pause between the two lines of the verse, create displacements in the original harmony. Corresponding passages between the two settings are still similar, but these passages no longer occur in exactly the same place (see examples 3a and 3b).[14]

These two versions of the *Quia respexit* imply that the *Magnificat à 6* has served as the model for the *Magnificat à 7* rather than vice versa. It seems more likely that the instruments were added to form the larger *Magnificat* rather than subtracted to form the smaller one. This supposition is supported by the differences in the bass lines underlying the plainchant, since several of the changes are necessitated by the presence of the *obbligato* instruments.

The parallels between the two *Magnificat*s in their first three verses yield to a reversal of styles and performing forces in the next two segments. In the *Magnificat à 6* the *Quia fecit* is set for six voices *in Dialogo,* i.e., in alternating groups of three voices. The two trios contrast in sonority, one comprising the three high voices with the plainchant in the topmost part, and the other the three low voices, likewise with the plainchant in the topmost part. The two trios alternate with each phrase of the text until the last, where they join together. Since the general stylistic character of the trios resembles late sixteenth-century polyphony, the setting has a decidedly conservative flavor despite the dialogue technique.

This conservative *Quia fecit* is followed by the *Et misericordia* in a modern duet style. Two virtuoso sopranos are concerted with the Magnificat-tone *cantus firmus* in the tenor in a setting similar to the *Et exultavit.*

EXAMPLE 3a. *Magnificat à 6, Quia respexit*

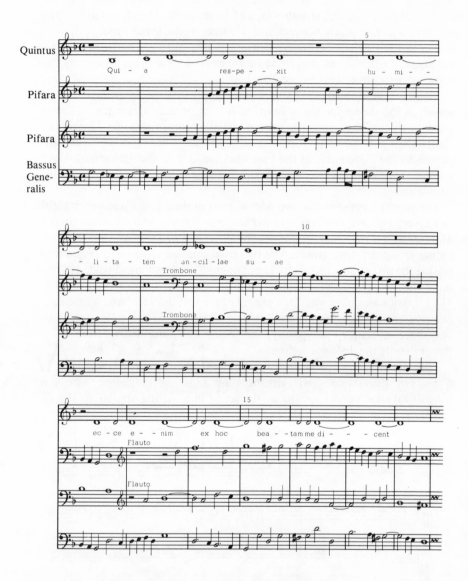

EXAMPLE 3b. *Magnificat à 7, Quia respexit*

In the *Magnificat à 7* the styles of the two verses are inverted. Here the *Quia fecit* is the virtuoso duet, now set for two basses with the alto carrying the *cantus firmus,* and the *Et misericordia* is the polyphonic dialogue in six parts. The *Quia fecit* employs *obbligato* instruments in addition to the voices and resembles the *Et misericordia* of the *Magnificat à 6* only in general character and overall structural outline: both pieces begin imitatively, reach a cadence in a major key in declamatory, chordal style, continue with only one of the duet parts (the small *Magnificat* also has the *cantus firmus* at this point), and then restore the voice pairing to the end.

Not only are the types of settings reversed between the two *Magnificats,* but in the six-voice dialogues, the position of each trio is inverted as well. The high trio comes first in the *Magnificat à 6,* but the low trio precedes in the *Magnificat à 7.* A reversal of tonal structure is also in evidence, for the *Quia fecit* of the smaller *Magnificat* rotates the Aeolian mode between G and D as the trios alternate, while the *Et misericordia* of the larger *Magnificat* oscillates in the opposite direction between D and G. Though a vague resemblance may be seen when comparing one trio with its counter-

EXAMPLE 4a. *Magnificat à 6, Quia fecit*

EXAMPLE 4b. *Magnificat à 7, Et misericordia*

part in the other *Magnificat,* there is no close identity between the two (see examples 4a and 4b).

Despite occasional similarities in the individual voices and the bass lines, the *Quia fecit-Et misericordia* pairs are not as closely related to one another as some of the other verses already discussed. The concept and structure of these segments are parallel in reverse order, but the details differ considerably.

In the succeeding verses Monteverdi's imagination appears inexhaustible in the variety of means he finds for adapting the settings of one *Magnificat* to the other. The *Fecit potentiam* of the *Magnificat à 6* calls for two sopranos with the alto intoning the *cantus firmus.* At first sight this would appear to bear little relation to the other *Fecit potentiam,* which is for three string instruments and *cantus firmus.* Moreover, the latter rendering is in triple meter while the former is in duple time. As in the *Quia respexit* settings, the version with *obbligato* instruments is a more extended piece. But once again the bass lines reveal a relationship, with substantial portions of the *Magnificat à 7* parallel to passages of the *Magnificat à 6.* This is illustrated in example 5, which distributes the bass from the larger *Magnificat* below that of the smaller one.

Once it is observed that the lowest of the three instruments in the *Magnificat à 7* merely doubles the continuo part, it becomes evident that the two violins are an instrumental substitute for the two sopranos from the *Magnificat à 6.* The violin parts are entirely different from the vocal lines, but they serve the same function in relation to the plainchant in the alto.

EXAMPLE 5. *Fecit potentiam,* bass lines

A similar substitution is manifest in the two *Deposuit*s. The *Magnificat à 6* again employs paired sopranos against the *cantus firmus,* which this time appears in the tenor. The sopranos engage in virtuoso ornamentation, alternating with one another "in echo" (see example 6a). The *Magnificat à 7* substitutes first two *cornetti* and later two violins for the sopranos and similarly treats them in echo fashion (see example 6b). Close parallels in the upper parts may be seen in comparing examples 6a and 6b, though such parallels are not pursued systematically. But like the *Fecit potentiam* settings, there are similarities between the two basses.

The two versions of the *Esurientes* provide another instance where an organ *ritornello* in the small *Magnificat* has been replaced by an instrumental *ritornello* in the larger one. The vocal parts of both settings consist simply of the plainchant in parallel thirds, sung by alto and tenor in the *Magnificat à 6* and sopranos in the *Magnificat à 7*. The *Magnificat à 6* maintains triple meter throughout, while the *Magnificat à 7* alternates between triple and duple meter for the *ritornelli* and the chant. The *ritornelli* themselves are quite different from one setting to the other, but in both versions the verse appears without continuo accompaniment until near the end.

EXAMPLE 6a. *Magnificat à 6, Deposuit*

EXAMPLE 6b. *Magnificat à 7, Deposuit*

Although the two *Magnificat*s have displayed rather close parallels
through their first eight sections, the next verse, *Suscepit Israel,* is subjected
to two completely different treatments. The small *Magnificat* follows the
pattern of the preceding *Esurientes*. The *cantus firmus* is in parallel thirds
again, this time for two sopranos, and the organ performs a *ritornello* that
joins the voices for the last two words of the text. As in the *Esurientes,* the
organ does not otherwise sound while the voices are singing.

The *Suscepit Israel* of the large *Magnificat* also employs two sopranos,
but in a virtuoso duet over a tenor *cantus firmus*. There is no *ritornello*
structure and the basso continuo of this version bears no relationship to the
bass of the other.

With the succeeding *Sicut locutus est* Monteverdi returns to the parody
process, once more substituting instruments in the large *Magnificat* for
voices of the smaller one. The *Magnificat à 6* is set for five parts, with four
of the voices arranged in a dialogue between a soprano-bass pair and a
soprano-tenor pair, the latter repeating precisely the phrases of the former.
The middle register is occupied by the alto intoning the *cantus firmus*.

The version with instruments in the *Magnificat à 7* juxtaposes a pair of violins with a pair of *cornetti* (the organ bass is also doubled alternately by a viola and a trombone), but the *cantus firmus* is still in the alto and there is a strong resemblance between the bass lines of the two segments (see examples 7a and 7b). An especially rapid exchange in the dialogue of the small *Magnificat* even finds a parallel in the instrumental dialogue of the other setting (see examples 8a and 8b). Once again a similarity between the two basses may be noted.

EXAMPLE 7a. *Magnificat à 6, Sicut locutus est*

EXAMPLE 7b. *Magnificat à 7, Sicut locutus est*

EXAMPLE 8a. *Magnificat à 6, Sicut locutus est*

EXAMPLE 8b. *Magnificat à 7, Sicut locutus est*

In the first verse of the Doxology, the *Gloria Patri,* one encounters for only the second time a substantial difference in concept between the two *Magnificat*s. Though both settings are highly melismatic, the smaller *Magnificat* employs the full six-voice chorus. This polyphonic texture is periodically interrupted by repetition of phrases of the text in unadorned plainchant in only one voice, the alternation continuing to the end.

The *Gloria Patri* of the *Magnificat à 7* is yet another trio texture, with the Magnificat-tone *cantus firmus* in the soprano accompanied by a virtuoso duet for two tenors, the second frequently responding in echo to the first.

In the final verse, the *Sicut erat,* the two *Magnificat*s once again resemble each other closely. Both employ a full polyphonic texture with the *cantus firmus* in the top part. There are several passages where the bass lines are similar, but the setting *à 7* is somewhat extended, both in the verse itself and the concluding *Amen.* The larger *Magnificat* also calls for full instrumental doubling of the voices, forming a full-sounding, grandiose conclusion to the entire composition as well as to the complete Vesper service.[15]

The variety and ingenuity displayed in Monteverdi's adaptations of the verse settings from one canticle to the other are impressive. Although he has maintained basic similarities in ten of the twelve sections, each of these verses has been modified in a substantial manner. His procedure is unquestionably parodistic, but since each of the *Magnificat* segments is based on the same plainchant *cantus firmus,* there is often little difference between the parody process from one *Magnificat* to the other and the process of variation as it unfolds in the successive sections of a single *Magnificat.* The transformation of a virtuoso soprano duet with *cantus firmus* in one *Magnificat* into a duet for instruments with *cantus firmus* in the other is essentially the same procedure as accompanying the *cantus firmus* with a virtuoso tenor duet in one verse of a canticle and a virtuoso bass duet in another verse of the same composition. Because of the constant presence of the *cantus firmus,* correspondences in the basses of *different* verses of each *Magnificat* can also be observed. They do not approach the frequency of resemblances between parallel settings in the two *Magnificat*s, however, since Monteverdi's parody technique creates closer relationships than his variations. The difference between parody and variation in the *Magnificat*s is thus a question of similarity between two compositions versus variety within a single piece. This distinction is a matter of degree, not a dissimilarity in basic process or concept, and it is doubtful if the semantic separation made today from a historical perspective existed in Monteverdi's mind. In both cases he was working with a musical constant, which he continually altered or adapted in some manner to a new context. Thus, by describing the details of Monteverdi's parody process, most aspects of his variation technique within each *Magnificat* have also been discerned, and only a brief commentary on the *cantus firmus* itself and its effect on harmony and tonality remains to be added.

The Magnificat chant chosen by Monteverdi is Tone 1, beginning on F and concluding on D.[16] However, Monteverdi also frequently transposes the tone up a fourth so that the concluding note of the chant is G, as in the opening and closing segments of both compositions. These two levels often alternate, but not consistently. In both *Magnificat*s the transposed version is more common, and the primary notated tonality of both canticles is G minor. But with the recitation tone falling at times on D, at times on A, there is also opportunity for modulation to B-flat, D minor, and F major. Because the plainchant is always sung in relatively long note values, there is room for substantial harmonic variety within any given tonality. Indeed, Monteverdi achieves remarkable diversity in the bass lines harmonizing parallel passages of the chant in the successive sections of each *Magnificat.* But despite such variety, certain similarities between the basses of different sections do exist. The virtuoso duets, for example, all tend to have slow-moving, strongly cadential basses. Basses consisting of ascending and descending scales are also common, and as noted above, more detailed similarities between the basses of parallel passages in different verses occasionally arise as well.

At this point it is appropriate to inquire why only ten of the twelve sections of the two *Magnificat*s are parallel and why Monteverdi has chosen to reverse the settings of two successive segments from one *Magnificat* to the other. The answer appears to depend on structural considerations and reinforces the hypothesis that the *Magnificat à 6* served as the model for the *Magnificat à 7*. In the *Magnificat à 6* the sections proceed with a judicious eye for variety of texture and style, but no overall structural pattern emerges from the sum of the twelve verses. With the reversal of the settings for the *Quia fecit-Et misericordia* pair and newly composed settings for the *Suscepit Israel* and *Gloria Patri,* the segments of the *Magnificat à 7* fall into a symmetrical ordering based both on style and the use of *obbligato* instruments (see diagram I).[17] Therefore it seems that Monteverdi, in modelling one *Magnificat* upon the other, also sought to impose a more balanced, large-scale structural organization on his second effort. If so, it is apparent that in using parody techniques in both the respond and the *Magnificat*s, it was Monteverdi's tendency to elaborate and expand upon his models rather than to reduce them. This inclination to enlargement can be seen on the smaller scale of individual passages and sections as well as on the larger level of entire pieces.

Besides the *Magnificat*s, the only other composition in the Vespers employing a repeated *cantus firmus* in long note values is the *Sonata sopra Sancta Maria*. This work borrows the opening phrase from the Litany of the Saints and reiterates it in the soprano voice eleven times over a sonata for eight instruments.[18] The *cantus firmus* does not begin until well into the piece, and its successive statements are altered rhythmically and separated

DIAGRAM I

Magnificat	Chorus followed by solo soprano
Et exultavit	Virtuoso duet for tenors
Quia respexit	*Ritornello* structure and paired *obbligato* instruments
Quia fecit	Virtuoso duet for basses with two *obbligato* violins
Et misericordia	Two vocal trios in dialogue
Fecit potentiam	Duet for violins
Deposuit	Echo duets for *cornetti* and violins
Esurientes	*Ritornello* structure with Magnificat tone in parallel thirds in two voices
Suscepit Israel	Virtuoso duet for sopranos
Sicut locutus	Dialogue between paired *obbligato* instruments
Gloria Patri	Virtuoso duet for tenors
Sicut erat	Chorus

by rests of varying durations. Against the *cantus firmus* the instrumental sonata unfolds in several large sections with the first one restated at the end in the manner of a *da capo*. As in the *Magnificats*, the separate sections of the *Sonata* are in different styles and textures, and the meter frequently shifts between duple and triple. Unlike the *Magnificats*, the sections do not correspond with each restatement of the *cantus firmus,* for a single section may support several intonations of the chant melody.

Nevertheless, the concept of variation is indeed at work in the *Sonata,* concentrating specifically on rhythmic and melodic variation. The first two sections, for example, consist of the same material, first in duple meter, then recast in triple meter and reorchestrated, a procedure frequently encountered in dance pairs of the sixteenth and seventeenth centuries (see examples 9a and 9b).

EXAMPLE 9a. *Sonata sopra Sancta Maria*

EXAMPLE 9b. *Sonata sopra Sancta Maria*

A later figure, played by the violins in duet, is presented in several melodic and rhythmic variants, even in its first appearance: a scale in dotted eighths and sixteenths is embellished with an extra sixteenth and then continues in a sequence of ornamented broken thirds (see example 10).

The scalar pattern, in both melody and bass, is a fundamental motive in the *Sonata* and appears in a variety of guises (see examples 11a, 11b, and 11c). While variation procedures may be at the root of some of these similarities, others may be attributed to a basic motivic consistency throughout the composition. The figure shown in example 11c not only involves scalar motion, but also is closely related by inversion to the opening motive of the *Sonata* quoted in example 9a. In fact, the section based on this motive functions as a transition between the scalar forms of examples 11a and 11b and a new triple-meter section whose main motive bears a

EXAMPLE 10. *Sonata sopra Sancta Maria*

EXAMPLE 11a, b, c. *Sonata sopra Sancta Maria,* scalar basses

EXAMPLE 12. *Sonata sopra Sancta Maria*

strong resemblance to the opening figure (see example 12). An affinity with the sixth and seventh bars of example 10 may also be discerned.

The motive in example 12 undergoes several metamorphoses in the course of this section, but all its forms are sufficiently related to one another and to the opening motive in their use of conjunct and disjunct thirds to render perfectly natural and convincing the *da capo* return of the opening passage following the conclusion of this extended section.

These techniques in the *Sonata* illustrate the close relationship between Monteverdi's concepts of melodic and rhythmic variation and sixteenth-century methods of motivic development. Although the motives quoted in examples 9-12 are typical of the early seventeenth century in the strength and regularity of their rhythms and the time intervals of their imitations, the metamorphosis of one motive out of another by means of expansion, contraction, inversion, retrogression, and alteration of rhythmic values is the same process found in innumerable *ricercari* and *canzone* of the second half of the *Cinquecento*. It is only in those passages where greater identity of material is maintained, such as example 9, that one can speak of variation in the modern formal sense rather than thematic development. Yet the distinction between the two in the *Sonata sopra Sancta Maria* is largely a matter of degree, although it has significant structural implications. The techniques of thematic development facilitate the construction of large continuous sections, which maintain a certain sense of homogeneity despite alterations in the melodic material. The process of variation, on the other hand, through its retention of a basic and readily perceptible morphological identity, tends to subdivide the music into comparatively short, discrete sections where first one variation technique is exposed and then another. This is apparent in the first part of the *Sonata,* which relies more on the process of variation and is more highly sectionalized than those portions depending on sixteenth-century methods of motivic development.

A rather different approach to the treatment of a *cantus firmus* emerges in the hymn *Ave maris stella*. Here the harmonized plainchant is subjected to variations in texture and/or sonority in each successive verse. In all seven stanzas the chant melody is in the topmost voice (either a soprano or tenor), though it is cast in two slightly different metric and rhythmic versions (see example 13). Separating the second through sixth verses is an instrumental *ritornello*.

EXAMPLE 13. *Ave maris stella*, chant melody

The variation in texture and sonority derives primarily from the accompaniment to the chant. The first and last stanzas are identical eight-voice, double-choir polyphonic settings. The second and third stanzas reset the *cantus firmus* in triple meter and are musically identical to one another. However, the second verse is to be sung by the first four-voice choir and the third verse by the second choir. The fourth, fifth, and sixth verses retain the triple-meter version of the melody, but are performed by a solo voice with only basso continuo support. The solo voice itself changes from stanza to stanza: the fourth verse is assigned to a soprano from the first chorus (*Cantus* part), the fifth to a soprano from the second chorus (*Sextus* part), and the sixth to a tenor in the first chorus (*Tenor* part). Throughout all seven stanzas the basic harmonization of the plainchant remains unchanged.[19]

The techniques of variation encountered in the compositions with the plainchant in long note values are relatively simple when compared to the multitude and complexity of variation procedures in the five psalms. In the psalms the problem is complicated by rhythmic values in the chant equivalent to the other voices and by the static nature of the psalm tone itself. The Magnificat tone, the litany, and the hymn all have some melodic interest, thereby facilitating variety in the harmonization of the chant. But the psalm tone, with its almost constant reiteration of a single pitch, imposes severe harmonic restrictions on the composer. The multiplicity of ways in which Monteverdi has resolved this problem is a major testament to his genius.

Each of the five psalms is structured around the psalm tone in a different manner. The first psalm, *Dixit Dominus,* has a largely symmetrical

DIAGRAM II

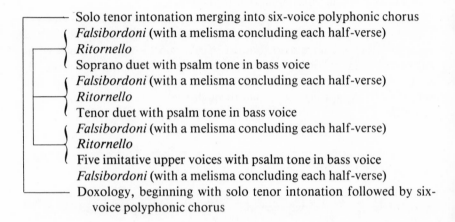

Solo tenor intonation merging into six-voice polyphonic chorus
Falsibordoni (with a melisma concluding each half-verse)
Ritornello
Soprano duet with psalm tone in bass voice
Falsibordoni (with a melisma concluding each half-verse)
Ritornello
Tenor duet with psalm tone in bass voice
Falsibordoni (with a melisma concluding each half-verse)
Ritornello
Five imitative upper voices with psalm tone in bass voice
Falsibordoni (with a melisma concluding each half-verse)
Doxology, beginning with solo tenor intonation followed by six-voice polyphonic chorus

organization, most segments of which correspond with a verse of the text (see diagram II).

In the opening polyphonic section the psalm tone, moving primarily in minims and semiminims, is combined with a second subject in an imitative texture. The symmetrically placed Doxology begins with a slow intonation of the chant by the tenor alone, transposed down a step to *g,* but in the concluding *Sicut erat* the long-note *cantus firmus* moves to *d* in the bass, creating a mostly static harmonic foundation. Above this bass the upper parts revolve around the pitches of the D minor triad in five-voice polyphony. As a result, the *Sicut erat* has the character of rhythmically enlivened *falsobordone,* not unlike *Domine ad adiuvandum.* With the transposition of the recitation tone to *d,* the primary harmony is based on the same tonic as the respond.

Between these two framing sections the series of *falsibordoni, ritornelli,* and thinner imitative textures unfolds. The *falsibordoni* consist of unrhythmicized chordal settings of the recitation tone, harmonized alternately in each of the verses as the third of A minor and G major triads. The soprano duet, tenor duet, and five-voice imitative passage all comprise different variations over a *cantus firmus* bass with the recitation tone notated mostly in minims and semiminims. In the two duets each half-verse begins with a single voice accompanied by a largely stationary continuo. The imitative second part is introduced by repetition of the text, while the bass voice simultaneously transforms the static continuo into a rhythmicized recitation tone. Thus repetition of each half-verse prompts a variation in its setting. A subtle coloristic variation is also achieved by shifting the leading role from one voice to the other for the second half of each verse.

In each of the tripartite sections outlined above, only the optional *ritornello* and the melisma concluding each passage of *falsobordone* are free of the psalm tone. Even these melismas are based on the concept of variation, with each melisma a different rhythmic form of the same basic descending sequence (three of eight variants are shown in examples 14a, 14b, and 14c).[20] Each *ritornello* is similarly a slightly modified repetition (transposed up a step) of the immediately preceding melisma, exchanging the vocal sonority for an instrumental one.

The beginning of the Doxology, where the tenor carries the chant in long notes supported solely by the continuo, offers yet another approach to the *cantus firmus*. The subsequent *Sicut erat,* with the *cantus firmus* in the bass as described above, is thus a variant on the *Gloria Patri* in harmonizing the chant with full chorus rather than continuo alone. In performance, if the optional *ritornelli* are played, the instruments could also be used to double the voices in this concluding choral passage, creating further variety in sonority.

The second psalm, *Laudate pueri,* is for eight-voice choir, but Monteverdi rarely divides the ensemble into antiphonal four-voice groupings, showing a much stronger inclination to pair voices in the same register.[21] Throughout this piece the composer is extremely flexible in his treatment of the plainchant. The psalm tone migrates freely from voice to voice, is

EXAMPLE 14a. *Dixit Dominus,* melisma

EXAMPLE 14b. *Dixit Dominus,* melisma

EXAMPLE 14c. *Dixit Dominus,* melisma

transposed several times and is absent altogether in some passages. Nevertheless, each verse of the psalm appears at least once in plainchant.

The opening of *Laudate pueri* develops similarly to the beginning of *Dixit Dominus,* for after a brief initial solo intonation, the psalm tone combines with a second motive to evolve a steadily expanding imitative texture. After the first verse, where *Dixit Dominus* turns to the tripartite series of *falsibordoni, ritornelli,* and duets, *Laudate pueri* proceeds with a lengthy succession of virtuoso duets for equal voices accompanied by the *cantus firmus.* In this section of the piece the chant migrates with each verse to the *Quintus, Altus, Cantus,* and *Sextus,* before dropping out entirely near the beginning of the final duet. The psalm tone appears both in long notes and in quicker minims and semiminims, but even in its faster rhythmic values the *cantus firmus* appears sustained because of the rapid embellishments in the other voices. The movement of the chant out of the low register to the upper parts, where it no longer forms the bass, permits increased harmonic variety, and two successive transpositions of the psalm tone upward by a fifth in verses 2-4 admit a wider tonal compass as well. These migrations and transpositions bring the *cantus firmus* to the top of the vocal texture at the climactic verse, "The Lord is high above all nations, and his glory above the heavens." As the psalm text gradually turns back toward humanity, the chant returns to its original tonal level and step by step migrates back through the voices to the *Tenor* and *Quintus.*[22]

The duet variations on the *cantus firmus* encompass verses 2-6, but from verse 7, *Suscitans a terra,* to the Doxology, the chant is embedded in a fuller choral texture, appearing in a different voice in each verse (*Altus, Quintus,* and finally *Tenor*). Temporary absences of the psalm tone in each of these verses allow even further harmonic flexibility. In verse 8 Monteverdi twice arrives at a semi-cadence on an E major triad, which would have been impossible were the chant sounding at those moments. Since the *cantus firmus* never returns to the lowest voice, it never completely governs the harmony. Although the recitation tone is consistently on *c'* from verse 7 to the end, the harmonization may be in either C major or A minor. Cadences in G major also occur in this section, which is generally characterized by substantial tonal variety. The texture likewise varies considerably, with the style ranging from chordal to imitative and the number of voices changing constantly.

The Doxology constitutes still another variation in the treatment of the plainchant. In the *Gloria Patri,* after an initial polyphonic statement without *cantus firmus,* the recitation tone is presented in the *Quintus* (second tenor) with continuo support only, reminiscent of the corresponding passage in *Dixit Dominus.* The chant is in sustained notes rather than the shorter values used earlier and alternates with a brief chordal passage in triple meter, which is treated antiphonally. The *Sicut erat,* as in many psalms of the late sixteenth and early seventeenth centuries, derives from its text, "as it was in the beginning," the rationale for a varied repetition of the opening music of the psalm, employing the same motives in new combinations and a compressed format (these motives, in varied form, also serve to introduce the *Gloria Patri*). The extended polyphonic *Amen* forms an entirely separate coda and abjures the plainchant altogether.

The variation procedures and formal structure in *Laetatus sum* do not depend on the psalm tone at all, but rather on the disposition of the text. In this piece the plainchant appears only occasionally in a tenor, alto, or soprano voice, although it does stand out prominently when it is used. Instead of the *cantus firmus*, the framework for variation is a series of independent bass patterns, which are repeated in the sequence ABACD, ABACD, ABD. Each pattern corresponds to one verse of the text except C and D, which combine for a single verse. The *Sicut erat,* concluding the Doxology, coincides with the final statement of pattern D.

The first of these structural modules is the famous walking bass frequently cited in the Monteverdi literature (see example 15a).[23] This bass is repeated verbatim in each of its five recurrences, lending the psalm a strong sense of harmonic and structural continuity. The varied reiteration of the other three patterns has generally escaped notice (see examples 15b, 15c, and 15d).[24] The systematic return of these basses tightens the organization of the composition even further.

The walking bass is both highly repetitive and sequential in its motivic structure. The second bass pattern (example 15b) is similarly repetitive. The

EXAMPLE 15a, b, c, d. *Laetatus sum,* bass patterns

third unit (example 15c), however, is almost completely static and serves as the support for virtuoso passagework both times it appears. The last pattern (example 15d) is also repetitious in that the final four bars are a sequential replication of the preceding four. The virtuoso passagework over pattern C introduces verses 4 and 8, which then continue with a more normal polyphonic texture over pattern D.

Although these patterns are on the surface very different from one another, there are some important points of similarity among three of the four. A comparison between the beginning of the walking bass and pattern B demonstrates that the latter is a slower moving variant of the former, particularly in its harmonic outline (see example 16). The fourth bass also uses scalar motives similar to the first and second. Only pattern C, without any rhythmic or pitch motion at all, is radically different.

EXAMPLE 16. *Laetatus sum,* bass relationships

The structural sequence of these patterns, as schematized above, gives special prominence to the walking bass, which underlies every other verse until the Doxology. The other basses are all varied somewhat upon repetition, but without obscuring their fundamental identities. The entire psalm, therefore, unfolds as a complex series of strophic variations, inspired perhaps by Monteverdi's essays in strophic variation in *L'Orfeo.* There too the composer frequently varied the bass lines in each successive strophe.

Monteverdi's ingenuity in writing strophic variations is readily apparent in the manifold ways he manipulates the six voices, achieving astonishing variety in texture and style as a counterbalance to the repetitive character of the supporting parts. A few examples from the walking-bass sections will suffice to illustrate this variety (see examples 17a, 17b, and 17c). Nevertheless, there is still a tendency to parallelism among sections on the same bass, especially obvious in the florid passages built over a sustained pitch. Each statement of the walking bass supports a progressively larger number of upper parts. The fourth pattern normally underlies a full six-voice choral sonority, while the second bass, itself substantially altered in its third appearance, forms the foundation for three different textures in the upper voices. The sporadic, though prominent, statements of the plainchant occur in connection with all of these basses, sometimes in the prevailing rhythms and sometimes as a long-note *cantus firmus.* During the sustained-note sections, the psalm tone forms a pedal fifth over the bass note.

EXAMPLE 17a. *Laetatus sum,* walking bass

EXAMPLE 17b. *Laetatus sum,* walking bass

Nisi Dominus is constructed in a wholly different manner from the preceding three psalms. Two five-voice choirs combine in dense polyphony at the beginning and end, but alternate as strict *cori spezzati* in the central portion of the composition. The tenor of each choir intones the *cantus firmus* ceaselessly throughout the entire piece. At times the chant is in longer notes than the other parts, but it also frequently moves at the same speed. In order to allow for harmonic variety, Monteverdi includes both the *initium* and the *terminatio* in each restatement of the *cantus firmus* rather than merely repeating the recitation tone after the opening. Example 18 illustrates the variety of harmony Monteverdi's bass is able to achieve because of this. Even so, midway through the psalm, at *Sicut sagittae,* the tone is transposed up a fourth, allowing harmonization in B-flat and G

EXAMPLE 17c. *Laetatus sum,* walking bass

EXAMPLE 18. *Nisi Dominus*

minor in contrast to the predominating F major and D minor of the preceding sections. At the beginning of the Doxology the tone is transposed back down a fifth, permitting harmonization in E-flat major and C minor before returning to its original level for the *Sicut erat.*

Aside from this tonal variety, the main force for variation in *Nisi Dominus* is rhythm. There is continual change in the rhythmic organization from one passage to the next, with many sections possessing a lively dance-like character. Triple meter relieves the prevailing duple time during the verses where the psalm tone is transposed to B-flat, and even in duple meter

EXAMPLE 19. *Nisi Dominus* (cont. on next page)

there are passages in which melodic phrases are clearly organized in groups of three minims (see example 19).

The structural organization of *Nisi Dominus* does not coincide precisely with the verses of the text as they are subdivided in the Vulgate. Monteverdi, rather, follows the sentence structure of the psalm in disposing both the *cantus firmus* and the two choirs, the second of which acts as a direct echo to the first in the central body of the piece.[25] The alternation of the choirs involves comparatively lengthy passages, but after the psalm tone is trans-

EXAMPLE 19 continued.

posed at *Sicut sagittae,* the exchanges proceed at a more rapid rate, leading
to the recombination of the two ensembles in the next verse. The Doxology
commences with the shift to E-flat major noted above, but the *Sicut erat*
recapitulates almost precisely the opening of the psalm with only a brief
Amen added at the conclusion.[26]

The straightforward use of the plainchant and the uncomplicated structural and tonal scheme of *Nisi Dominus* are succeeded by a more complex
treatment in the last psalm, *Lauda Jerusalem.* This piece is also charac-

terized by frequent antiphonal responses and an almost continuous *cantus firmus* in the tenor, but the texture is thinner, comprising only seven voices. The six parts aside from the tenor subdivide into two equal ensembles of soprano, alto, and bass, and the resulting transparent sonorities facilitate more frequent interchanges and greater rhythmic complexity than in *Nisi Dominus*.

Lauda Jerusalem progresses uninterruptedly without repetitions or symmetry, although each successive verse is marked by a cadence and shift in the texture. After an opening that alternates a full chordal sound with the unadorned psalm tone, the chant continues pervasively with only occasional short breaks at the *mediatio* or between the verses. The recitation tone, which is *c'* for the first three verses, is harmonized with both C major and A minor (cadences frequently occur on A major triads).[27] In verses 4-6 the chant is transposed up a fourth, permitting harmonization in F major and D minor, but in verses 7-9 the *cantus firmus* returns to its original level. The Doxology reveals a similar process, as explained below. Within the prescribed tonal areas the harmony fluctuates continually, never establishing any distinctive patterns.

While the tonal movement in this psalm is a function of the level at which the recitation tone appears, structure on a smaller scale is determined by antiphony as in *Nisi Dominus*. In *Lauda Jerusalem,* however, the exchanges between the ensembles occur much more rapidly. Instead of responding with antiphonal echoes, each ensemble contributes to the textual and musical continuity. The antiphonal exchanges initially proceed at regular time intervals, but with the fifth verse the time span is reduced by half. Finally the two groups join in verse 7, at the point where the chant returns to its original level, remaining combined until the Doxology. Although this full-voiced passage is mostly chordal, it is simultaneously imitative at very short time intervals, producing a lively mosaic of entrances as pitches and motives first heard in one trio reappear almost immediately in the other.

Only the Doxology is treated as a separate section. For the first time the chant migrates out of the tenor into the top voice, achieving greater prominence. During the *Gloria Patri*, where the *cantus firmus* is once again transposed up a fourth, all voices are slower moving, but for the *Sicut erat* the recitation tone returns to C and the prevailing rhythms are restored (the reciting tone is also briefly transposed to E in this section). Unlike *Nisi Dominus*, the *Sicut erat* of *Lauda Jerusalem* differs from the opening of the psalm. Here the passage resembles measured *falsobordone* with occasional ornamental elaboration and staggering of the various parts. A large polyphonic *Amen,* in which the *cantus firmus* is for the first time absent, concludes what must be described as a through-composed setting of the psalm text.

These five psalms demonstrate Monteverdi's inexhaustible imagination and ingenuity. The melodically monotonous psalm tone, rather than proving restrictive, stimulated Monteverdi to a multitude of divergent solutions, most of them rooted in the process of variation. In these settings variations in vocal style, variations in texture, variations in choral and solo sonorities, variations over ground basses, tonal variation, harmonic variation, melodic variation, rhythmic variation, and variation in antiphonal effects all come into play. Yet the psalm tones and the limitations they impose serve as a binding thread for all five compositions, generating aesthetic consistency and cohesion despite the diversity of treatments. These psalms highlight two opposite but complementary facets of Monteverdi's genius. Not only does his imagination appear boundless, but he is also a disciplined master of formal design. Without the carefully planned structures based on the psalm tones, symmetry, and variation schemes, the enormous diversity of styles and techniques would have produced only a series of loose fragments lacking plausible relationships to one another. By the same token, without the variety of remarkably imaginative treatments of the psalm tone, the most tightly planned structural organization would not have saved these pieces from monotony. This combination of freedom of imagination and organizational discipline is an artistic achievement of the highest order, palpably distinguishing Monteverdi from his contemporaries.

The remaining four pieces of the Vespers, the motets *Nigra sum, Pulchra es, Duo Seraphim,* and *Audi coelum,* are all in the modern solo or few-voice style and are without any dependence on a *cantus prius factus.* Nevertheless, an examination of these works demonstrates once again that variation techniques are basic to Monteverdi's compositional process.

Of the variation procedures employed in the motets, melodic variation is of particular interest. *Pulchra es,* set for two sopranos, begins with only one voice, the other not appearing until the eighth bar (see example 20). When the *Sextus* enters, it opens with the same melody Monteverdi had already notated on the upper staff of the *partitura* at the beginning.[28] But while this

EXAMPLE 20. *Pulchra es*

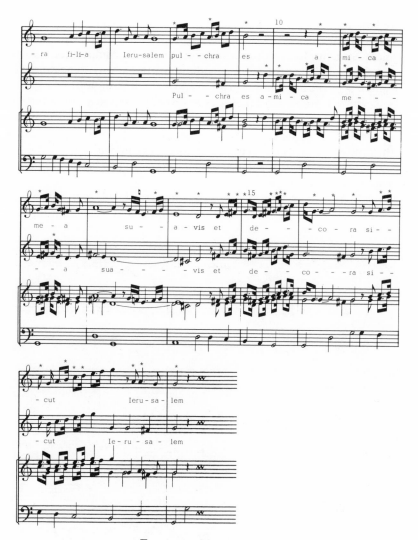

EXAMPLE 20 continued.

melody had originally served as a countersubject to the *Cantus* in bars 1-2, it is simultaneously a melodic variation upon it, as indicated by the asterisks in the *Sextus* part in the example. The continuation of the *Sextus* in bars 11-14 prolongs the melodic variation, which is further enhanced by the anticipatory fragment in the *Cantus* in bar 8 and the subsequent imitative entrance in the latter part of bar 10. The *Cantus* persists with a further melodic variation in bars 14-18, corresponding to bars 5-7, again marked by asterisks.

The bass line of bars 8-18 is virtually identical to that of bars 1-7, the repetition in bar 11 being necessitated by the presence of the two voices in imitation. Structurally, therefore, this portion of the composition can appropriately be designated AA´, the addition of the *Sextus* coinciding with the beginning of the harmonic repetition and melodic variation.

The *Sextus* is used later in *Pulchra es* to forge a variation in sonority coincident with another structural repetition. From the verse *Averte oculos tuos* to the conclusion of the text, the composition reverts to the solo *Cantus*. But then the entire section is repeated almost verbatim with the addition of the *Sextus* in parallel thirds and occasional counterpoint with the *Cantus*, at times above, at times below it.

Melodic variation in the motets does not always coincide with bass repetition. The melodic organization of *Audi coelum* exhibits cohesion through

EXAMPLE 21a, b. *Audi coelum*

EXAMPLE 22. *Audi coelum*

the use of variation *despite* the absence of sectional repetition and parallel bass patterns. Examples 21a and 21b compare two obviously related melodic fragments, but their basses are completely different and the two examples are even in different keys. Further expansion and elaboration of the same basic melodic shape follows in a later passage (see example 22). In fact, bars 20-31, quoted in part in example 22, may be described as a free melodic variation of bars 9-19, which begin with the passage in example 21b. While the basses do not coincide in these two sections, there are nevertheless some similarities, especially with respect to parallel modulations.

Later in this motet the style turns to recitative and there appear three successive versions of the same declamatory phrase, finally concluding with a melismatic variant of the rise from *a* to *d '* with which the section began (see example 23, overleaf). In view of the fact that all of the passages discussed here are based on this rise from *a* to *d '*, expanded at times to *g* to *d '* or even *f* to *d '*, the beginning two bars of the motet are instructive with regard to Monteverdi's technique (see example 24). Here we have the motivic kernel out of which the melodic structure of the motet evolves. Monteverdi's procedure is to develop his motives freely, expanding and ornamenting them, but always preserving a fundamental relationship to the opening of the piece. Looking at the same issue in reverse, the initial motive may be considered a reduction to the simplest form of the most important melodic shapes of the composition.

EXAMPLE 24. *Audi coelum*

The repetition of a passage with variation in sonority is an important feature of *Audi coelum*, as it was in *Pulchra es*. But in *Audi coelum* the variant repetitions are effected by a second tenor in echo to the first rather than through sectional repeats. This second tenor echoes more softly, perhaps even at a spatial distance, the closing of several major phrases, forming a verbal pun on the concluding word of the first tenor (see example 25).

Melodic structuring similar to *Audi coelum* also characterizes *Nigra sum* and need not be discussed here in detail.[29] Note should be taken, however, of the use of melodic patterns in tonal sequences. Example 26 illustrates a descending melodic figure, first the fifth *d '* to *g,* then the fourth *d '* to *a,* which is repeated in varied and compressed forms at successively higher levels, modulating sequentially from G major to A minor to C major.

EXAMPLE 23. *Audi coelum*

Nigra sum also has an important structural repetition involving variation. The last section is reiterated with slightly varied vocal rhythm and an additional lengthy descending scale in the bass just before the end. This scale is designed to dissipate the energy and tension accumulated by the constant upward thrust of the melodic motion throughout the piece (see example 27).[30]

Techniques of construction in the three-voice *Duo Seraphim* are similar to the other motets. A few basic intervals serve as the outline for extraordinarily elaborate vocal ornamentation, and as in *Pulchra es*, the subsequent addition of a voice not present at the beginning begets variety in so-

EXAMPLE 25. *Audi coelum,* echo

EXAMPLE 26. *Nigra sum*

EXAMPLE 27. *Nigra sum*

nority. In *Duo Seraphim* the third tenor does not join the other two until the second part of the piece, prompted by the phrase *Tres sunt qui testimonium dant.* To conclude this second section, the last two lines of text from the first part are repeated to the same music. But in order to accommodate the additional tenor, the imitative texture is amplified in both length and density. This expansion produces an elongated and contrapuntally more complex variation on the corresponding passage in the first part of the motet.

For Monteverdi the concept of variation was obviously not limited to one or two fundamental procedures; rather it informs every aspect of his compositional process in the Vespers. Variations on the *cantus firmus* and repetitive basses forge the large-scale structural scaffolding of the psalms, *Magnificats*, hymn, and *Sonata sopra Sancta Maria*. Variation techniques are also at the heart of smaller structural formats in the psalms and motets. Variation in rhythm and sonority is a key factor in parallel passages throughout the Vespers. Melodic variation is one of the most important elements in the composition of the motets. Each of these general types of variation is manifested in a seemingly limitless variety of ways, and Monteverdi never employs exactly the same method twice. There is always some difference in approach, some difference in the intended effect.

Yet Monteverdi's variation procedures are in many instances not far removed from his parody process. The alterations that transform the toccata of *L'Orfeo* into the respond *Domine ad adiuvandum,* and the adaptations of the various sections of one *Magnificat* to the other are often quite similar to the variation techniques witnessed in other parts of the Vespers. Even the process of melodic and rhythmic variation is an extension of the simpler forms of paraphrase observed throughout the parody *Missa In illo tempore,* companion to the Vespers in the 1610 print.[31]

These concepts and procedures were new to Monteverdi in the years 1607-1610, for the much smaller genre of the madrigal did not require such structural considerations. In fact, aside from the mass, whose unifying techniques were evolved throughout the fifteenth and sixteenth centuries, there simply were no forms that demanded structural organization on such a large scale. The historical importance of *L'Orfeo* and the *Vespro della Beata Vergine* lies in part in the new architectural problems they posed. Monteverdi's awareness of these problems and his success in finding aesthetically convincing solutions not only testify to his remarkable ingenuity but also justify and reinforce his stature as a composer of extraordinary historical significance in the development of Western music.

NOTES

The musical examples in this chapter are adapted from the edition of G. Francesco Malipiero, *Tutte le opere di Claudio Monteverdi*, vol. xiv (Vienna: Universal Edition, 1932).

1. From 1604 through 1608 Monteverdi's letters are filled with complaints about difficulties in drawing his salary, overwork, ill health brought on by the Mantuan climate, and physical exhaustion. These complaints reach their climax in a bitter letter written to the court counselor Annibale Chieppo from Cremona on December 2, 1608, in which Monteverdi requests release from the ducal service. See G. Francesco Malipiero, *Claudio Monteverdi* (Milan: Fratelli Treves Editori, 1929), pp. 135-139, and Domenico De' Paoli, *Claudio Monteverdi: Lettere, Dediche e Prefazioni* (Rome: Edizioni de Santis, 1973), pp. 33-38. An English translation of this letter is found in Denis Arnold and Nigel Fortune, "The Man as seen through his Letters," *The Monteverdi Companion*, ed. Denis Arnold and Nigel Fortune (London: Faber and Faber, 1968), pp. 26-29. In addition to his financial difficulties, work load, and poor health, Monteverdi also suffered the death of his wife on September 10, 1607, and on March 9, 1608, the sudden death of the eighteen-year-old singer Caterina Martinella, who had been a boarder and student of Monteverdi's since 1603 and who was scheduled to sing the lead role in the imminent production of *Arianna*. Professional pressures on the composer arose not only from the Gonzaga court, but also through the attacks of the Bolognese theoretician Giovanni Maria Artusi, which Monteverdi felt compelled to rebut. This debate dragged on from 1600 to 1608. See Claude V. Palisca, "The Artusi-Monteverdi Controversy," *The Monteverdi Companion*, pp. 133-166. See also chapter I of this volume, p. 14, and chapter II, pp. 47-48 and 65.

2. Both the location and precise date of the first performance of *L'Orfeo* before the *Accademia degl'Invaghiti* in Mantua are unknown. The second performance took place in the ducal palace on February 24, 1607. See Guglielmo Barblan, Claudio Gallico, and Guido Pannain, *Claudio Monteverdi* (Turin: Edizioni RAI Radiotelevisione italiana, 1967), p. 47.

For the circumstances surrounding the first performance of *Arianna,* see Stuart Reiner, "La vag'Angioletta (and others)," *Analecta Musicologica* 14 (1974): 26-88. See also chapter I, p. 10 and note 8.

3. See chapter I, pp. 8-9.

4. See chapter I, pp. 10-11 and note 9.

5. Monteverdi's first extant letter, dated November 28, 1601, mentions some motets and masses that he had composed. See Malipiero, *Claudio Monteverdi,* pp. 127-128, and De' Paoli, *Claudio Monteverdi: Lettere, Dediche e Prefazioni,* pp. 17-18. An English translation is in Arnold and Fortune, *The Monteverdi Companion,* pp. 22-23. These lost items could hardly have been works in large quantities or of major significance since Monteverdi did not see fit to have them published. See chapter II, note 2 for my commentary on Don Siro Cisilino's publication of three anonymous masses under Monteverdi's name.

6. Monteverdi's first meeting with the librettist Rinuccini was on October 23, 1607. The project was originally scheduled for completion by Carnival in 1608. See Barblan et al., *Claudio Monteverdi,* pp. 51-52, and Reiner, "La vag'Angioletta."

7. See chapter I, pp. 9-12, for a detailed discussion of the circumstances surrounding the

composition and publication of the Mass and Vespers. A critical analysis of the Mass is found in chapter II.

8. See chapter V for an examination of the relationship between Monteverdi's Vespers and the contemporary sacred repertoire.

9. A discussion of the musical cohesion and integrity of the Vespers is found in my Ph.D. dissertation, "The Monteverdi Vespers of 1610 and their Relationship with Italian Sacred Music of the Early Seventeenth Century" (University of Illinois at Urbana-Champaign, 1972), pp. 194-248. A more updated view of tonal relationships in the Mass and Vespers, taking into consideration additional evidence, is found in chapter I of this volume, pp. 37-40.

10. See chapter V.

11. *Dixit Dominus, Ave maris stella,* and *Magnificat à 7.*

12. The voices are actually notated in unmeasured *falsobordone,* with the rhythm and text underlay given only in the *partitura.* See chapter I, p. 29. In the respond the trumpets of the *Orfeo* toccata are omitted and *cornetti* are assigned to double the violins.

13. Only Wolfgang Osthoff has called attention to the depth of these similarities. See Osthoff, "Unità liturgica e artistica nei 'Vespri' del 1610," *Rivista italiana di musicologia* 2, no. 2 (1967): 323, note 18. The most extensive study of the *Magnificat*s previously published is in Adam Adrio, *Die Anfänge des geistlichen Konzerts* (Berlin: Junker und Dünnhaupt Verlag, 1935), pp. 57-68. Adrio describes some striking resemblances between the two *Magnificat*s but attributes them to Monteverdi's representation of the text: *"dass der gegebene Text eine bestimmte klangliche Vorstellung des Komponisten hervorgerufen habe . . ."* (p. 64). Hans Redlich describes the *Magnificat à 6* as a "simplified 'pocket edition' of the preceding large Magnificat." See Redlich, *Claudio Monteverdi: Life and Works,* trans. Kathleen Dale (London: Oxford University Press, 1952), p. 129.

14. In bars 4-5 of example 3b the cadence in the bass is delayed by a half bar over example 3a in order to give the *pifare* a brief opportunity to sound alone. This displacement subsequently affects the bass in the succeeding bars. Bar 6 of example 3b compares with bars 5-6 of example 3a. Also compare bars 11-13 of example 3b with 10-12 of example 3a.

15. See chapter I, p. 36 for further discussion of instrumental doubling in the *Magnificat à 7.*

16. Both *Magnificat*s are notated in the high *chiavette.* For a discussion of the relationship between *chiavette,* transposition, and pitch, see chapter I, pp. 37-40.

17. For a similar diagram, but with comparisons made on the basis of number of voices alone, see Denis Stevens, "Where are the Vespers of Yesteryear?" *The Musical Quarterly* 47, no. 3 (July 1961): 330.

18. The Litany of the Saints is found in *The Liber Usualis with Introduction and Rubrics in English* (New York: Desclee Company, 1963), Appendix II, p. 2*.

19. Stevens diagrams the structural symmetry in the use of the two choirs in "Where are the Vespers of Yesteryear?" p. 330.

20. A number of closely related sequences can be found in the *Missa In illo tempore*. See Jerome Roche, "Monteverdi and the *Prima Prattica*," *The Monteverdi Companion,* pp. 173-174 and 176-178. See also chapter II of the present volume. Denis Arnold quotes a similar sequence from the sacred music of Giaches de Wert in his *Monteverdi,* revised ed. (London: J. M. Dent & Sons, Ltd., 1975), p. 134.

21. See chapter I, p. 30, for a discussion of the performance rubric of this psalm.

22. The full text of *Laudate pueri* reads as follows in the King James version (Psalm 113; 112 in the Vulgate): 1. Praise ye the Lord. Praise, O ye servants of the Lord, praise the name of the Lord. 2. Blessed be the name of the Lord from this time forth and for evermore. 3. From the rising of the sun unto the going down of the same the Lord's name is to be praised. 4. The Lord is high above all nations, and his glory above the heavens. 5. Who is like unto the Lord our God, who dwelleth on high. 6. Who humbleth himself to behold the things that are in heaven, and in the earth! 7. He raiseth up the poor out of the dust, and lifteth the needy out of the dunghill; 8. That he may set him with princes, even with the princes of his people. 9. He maketh the barren woman to keep house, and to be a joyful mother of children. Praise ye the Lord.

23. See in particular Denis Arnold's discussion of this bass in his "Formal Design in Monteverdi's Church Music," *Claudio Monteverdi e il suo Tempo, Atti del Congresso internazionale di Studi monteverdiani, May 3-May 7, 1968,* ed. Raffaello Monterosso (Verona: La Stamperia Valdonega, 1969), p. 207.

24. Hugo Leichtentritt has been the only one to outline the complexity of this repetitive structure. See Leichtentritt, *Geschichte der Motette,* reprint ed. after Leipzig 1908 ed. (Hildesheim: Georg Olms, 1967), p. 245. Jürgen Jürgens also mentions the repetition of three separate bass patterns in "Urtext und Affführungspraxis bei Monteverdis *Orfeo* und *Marien-Vesper,*" *Claudio Monteverdi e il suo Tempo,* p. 284.

25. The *Liber Usualis* subdivides the psalm text in the same manner as Monteverdi, resulting in a regular couplet structure and one more verse than enumerated in the Vulgate. Monteverdi's liturgical sources may have done the same because of the two-part structure of the psalm tone.

26. See chapter I, pp. 23-24, for a discussion of the conclusion of *Nisi Dominus*.

27. See the discussion of *chiavette* and transposition in *Lauda Jerusalem* in chapter I, pp. 37-40.

28. See the discussion of the *partitura* in chapter I, pp. 32-33.

29. For a detailed discussion of *Nigra sum* see chapter IV.

30. See chapter IV, p. 120.

31. For a full discussion of parody technique in the Mass, see chapter II.

CHAPTER IV

MELODIC STRUCTURE IN *NIGRA SUM*

Amid Monteverdi's correspondence there survive a number of letters written between 1618 and 1627 discussing various operatic projects. In these letters Monteverdi repeatedly stressed his need for adequate time in order to compose well rather than sloppily. Compositions completed in haste and performances insufficiently rehearsed troubled him greatly.[1] Indeed, it is becoming increasingly apparent to twentieth-century scholars that one of the main distinctions between the music of Monteverdi and that of his contemporaries is the carefully planned construction of his works, including even operatic recitatives. In his recitatives as well as in other monodies Monteverdi carefully adhered not only to the rhetorical expression and meaning of his texts but also to the necessities and requirements of purely musical logic.

The musical coherence of Monteverdi's *seconda pratica* compositions has often been overlooked by taking too literally his brother Giulio Cesare's famous declaration that in the new style "it has been his intention to make the words the mistress of the harmony and not the servant."[2] Monteverdi and his brother, for the sake of argument and because of a lack of enough time to develop the thesis at greater length, oversimplified the issue in the *Dichiaratione*. While Monteverdi certainly took the text as his point of departure as well as the ultimate rationale for many aspects of his madrigals, motets, and dramatic compositions, he never became a slavish imitator of words nor an ingenious inventor of musical metaphors after the fashion of Marenzio. In fact, Giulio Cesare's description of the *seconda pratica* may be said to apply more directly to Marenzio and Gesualdo than it does to Monteverdi.

Monteverdi's true goal, rather than the subservience of music to the text, was a balanced marriage of both textual and musical considerations, though this union took different forms in the recitative from the polyphonic and *concertato* madrigals and motets. But whatever the character of the composition, Monteverdi never ignored the demands of musical logic and coherence. Conversely, it is often this musical organization that gives the primary force to the expression of the text, for in the absence of a powerful musical

115

Nigra sum

logic, the addition of tone to word is likely to be unconvincing, inexpressive, and lacking in meaning.

Despite the success of his operas and the popularity of the Lament of Arianna, Monteverdi was not drawn frequently to monody *per se*, preferring instead the trio texture of two equal voices with basso continuo. Many of the pieces he did write for solo voice are set to sacred texts rather than secular poems. The earliest of these sacred monodies appears in the *Vespro della Beata Vergine* of 1610, published while the composer was still in the service of the Gonzaga court at Mantua. Two of the motets in this collection may be termed monodies: *Nigra sum,* in the purest sense of a single voice with continuo accompaniment, and *Audi coelum,* whose second tenor is confined solely to echoing the ends of phrases. *Audi coelum* is further complicated by the participation of a six-voice chorus in its concluding section.[3]

Nigra sum displays the kind of balance between musical logic and text expression that was at the heart of Monteverdi's *seconda pratica.* The text is drawn from several verses of the Song of Solomon, as is the text for another motet in the Vesper collection, the duet *Pulchra es.*[4] A translation of *Nigra sum,* based on the King James version, reads as follows:

> I am black, but comely,
> O ye daughters of Jerusalem.
> Therefore the king hath loved me
> and brought me into his chambers,
> and said unto me:
> Rise up, my love, my fair one, and come away!
> For, lo, the winter is past,
> the rain is over and gone;
> the flowers appear on the earth.
> The time of pruning is at hand.[5]

Monteverdi's designation of the tenor voice for this piece may seem odd in view of the first-person, feminine orientation of the text. If the motet were to be sung in church as part of a sacred service, however, it would have had to have been performed by a male singer, whatever the register in which it was composed. The choice of a tenor may in fact have been dictated by the specific singer Monteverdi had available for initial performances of the piece. It should be noted that two other motets in the Mass and Vesper print, *Duo Seraphim* and *Audi coelum*, are also for tenors.

On the other hand, if *Nigra sum* were to be performed outside of church, in "chapels or chambers of princes" according to one possibility suggested on Monteverdi's title page, it is conceivable that a female singer might have taken the part. We have no definite information as to whether the female vocalists so highly treasured as performers of secular music in the North Italian courts of this time might also have participated in private religious devotions. If they did, Monteverdi's designation of a tenor would have proved no barrier to performance by a woman, since it was common practice in the early seventeenth century to employ the tenor and *cantus* voices interchangeably. Countless published motets of the period carry the rubric *"canto ovvero tenore,"* and such a substitution may be assumed feasible even if the composer did not bother to indicate it.

To Monteverdi the essential concept of his text was embodied in the word *surge*. The command "arise" establishes the fundamental character and direction of the melodic construction throughout *Nigra sum*. At the very outset of the piece this rise is expressed in its simplest and most elemental form by means of an octave leap from the lower *d* to the higher *d'* (see bars 1-3 of the transcription). Monteverdi relieves this sudden, energetic beginning with a pair of descending motives in bars 3-4 and 4-7, first by a descent to *g* and then by a more leisurely descent to *a* which uses the *g* as a lower neighbor.

The energy originating from the first leap is at this point increased by yet a larger leap in bars 9-10 designed to enhance the upward thrust not only by its greater interval, but by arriving at a tone dissonant to the initial pitch. This *e'* in bar 10 also serves to announce the second stage of a rising tonal sequence encompassing bars 1-23. The sequence commences in G major and, beginning with the *e'*, rises to A minor in bars 11-14.

Now that the upward surge has been extended to the parameter of tonality as well as pitch and register, the third phrase completes the process by beginning at a higher pitch level with *Ideo* in bar 15 and rising to the highest note yet, the *f'* in bar 18, before continuing with the familiar short descending motive. This new pitch level coincides with the third stage of the tonal sequence, which is now in C major. These initial three phrases have thus established the generally upward direction of *Nigra sum*, first in an abrupt fashion with the opening leap and then more deliberately by the rising sequence of phrases passing from G major to A minor and finally C major.

The opening section of the motet does not conclude at this point, but is extended by a short *codetta* to accommodate the conjunctive phrase that introduces the next portion of the text: *et dixit mihi*. This brief *codetta* in bars 24-26 also serves as a melodic link between the two sections, diatonically filling the leap from *g* to *c'* with which the preceding phrase had begun (bars 15-17). This embellishment also anticipates the next section, which begins in bar 27 with an even more extended scalar ascent.

The second section begins at bar 27 with the word *surge* itself, which Monteverdi repeats several times accompanied by a variety of upward thrusts in the melody. At first the scale rises easily through a twelfth from the low *c* to the high *g'*, but then it turns back upon itself to settle on the *d'* in bar 31. This phrase may be considered a stepwise subdivision of the opening leap of the composition, expanded to a larger compass. The span between the *c* and *d'* at the beginning and end of the phrase effects a modulation back from C major, in which the first section closed, to the dominant of G, which was the harmony underlying the *d'* in bar 3. The upward drive of this phrase has also been enhanced by the continuo, following immediately behind the voice in imitation (bars 28-29).

Just as the octave rise at the outset of *Nigra sum* was accomplished deceptively simply with respect to its weighty significance in the composition as a whole, the ascent from *c* to *d'* in bars 27-31 has also occurred without great effort, even overshooting the mark by a fourth before resolving back to the principal tone. Monteverdi therefore retreats in bar 32 to the original *d* to attack the ascent more vigorously and systematically. First he repeats the rising scale, this time beginning on *d*, climbs only as far as *a*, and then settles on *g* (bars 32-34). The *g* next serves as the point of departure for a series of short sequential leaps reaching as high as *e'* in bar 36 before quickly coming back down again. This last phrase has brought the melody once more to the region of the upper *d'*, and in bar 38 Monteverdi begins his next phrase on the *d'* itself, hovering around this note throughout the recitative of the next eight bars. This circling around *d'* ascends as high as *f'* in bar 40, which was also the highest pitch at the climax of the sequence in the first section (bar 18). The prominence of *d'* is underscored by its repetition in bars 43-44 and the closure on *d'* in bar 46.

The entire passage from bars 27-46 can now be seen as a purposeful, methodical extension from the low *d* to the upper *d'*, a series of events foreshadowed in simple form in bars 1-3. Once the high *d'* has been attained in this systematic manner, Monteverdi emphasizes it decisively by the repetition of long sustained tones in bars 47-54. This recitation on *d'* fulfills and confirms the melodic goal of the composition. But to conclude at this point would have been unsatisfactory, for Monteverdi, in his continual upward drive, has constructed a powerful force and tension which are by no means resolved by the cadence in bars 55-56.

Monteverdi's solution to this dilemma is ingenious. He returns to bars 34-35 in the second section, repeating the sequential upward surge almost verbatim and reaching the high *d'* yet a second time. But in repetition this passage sounds slightly anticlimactic. Once the *d'* is attained again the bass begins an unprecedented downward scale, which is carried in a pair of sequential segments through almost two octaves (bars 69-74). This bass descent has the effect of quickly deflating and dissipating the accumulated energy and tension of the carefully calculated upward motion of the voice and now permits a satisfying closure almost identical in form to the unsatisfying cadence of bars 55-56.[6]

Nigra sum thus exemplifies an ideal union between poetry and music. Not only does Monteverdi carefully follow the rhythmic accents of the words and interpret their rhetorical inflections with corresponding inflections of pitch, but he has also conceived a melodic structure for the motet as a whole, pursued with relentless musical logic and yet derived from and in perfect harmony with the essential idea of the text. It should be little wonder that Monteverdi wished to "go slow" with his compositions in order that they be done well, for the marriage of poetic and musical meaning demonstrated here is the result of a deeply thoughtful process in which the composer has brought his greatest intellectual concentration to bear on the problems of his art.

NOTES

1. See in particular letters nos. 14, 15, 16, 19, 20, and 22 in Denis Arnold and Nigel Fortune, "The Man as Seen through his Letters," *The Monteverdi Companion* (London: Faber and Faber, 1968), pp. 48-62. Similar remarks are also found in other letters from this period not translated by Arnold and Fortune. See G. Francesco Malipiero, *Claudio Monteverdi* (Milano: Fratelli Treves Editori, 1929), letters nos. 38 and 49, pp. 187 and 205, and the more recent edition of the letters by Domenico De' Paoli, *Claudio Monteverdi: Lettere, Dediche e Prefazioni* (Rome: Edizioni de Santis, 1973), letters nos. 39 and 51, pp. 127-128 and 159-160.

2. The theory of the *seconda pratica* is propounded by Giulio Cesare Monteverdi in the famous *Dichiaratione* printed in the *Scherzi Musicali* of 1607. The *Dichiaratione* is cast in the form of extensive glosses upon the phrases of a *"Lettera"* that Claudio had printed in the Fifth Book of Madrigals of 1605 announcing his intention to publish a theoretical treatise explaining the rationale behind his "second practice." A modern edition of the *Dichiaratione* is found in Domenico De' Paoli, *Claudio Monteverdi: Lettere, Dediche e Prefazioni,* pp. 394-404. An English translation is in Oliver Strunk, *Source Readings in Music History* (New York: W. W. Norton & Co., Inc., 1950), pp. 405-412. The passage quoted here is on p. 406 in Strunk, but Giulio Cesare restates the same idea several times with different wording.

3. See chapter III, pp. 106-108 for a more extended discussion of *Audi coelum.*

4. In *Nigra sum*, Monteverdi adapts the Vulgate text by slightly rearranging it and mixing it with the third and fourth antiphons for Vespers on Feasts of the Blessed Virgin Mary. These antiphons had themselves originally been adapted from the Song of Solomon. The sources for both the antiphons and Monteverdi's text are chapter I, verses 2-4 and chapter II, verses 10-12.

5. Printed, among other places, in the liner notes of the Telefunken recording of the Vespers, SAWT 9501/02.

6. The ABB' structure of *Nigra sum* coincides with one of the most ubiquitous forms for small-scale secular and sacred works throughout the sixteenth and early seventeenth centuries. This fact does not contradict the conclusions drawn here, but rather underscores Monteverdi's genius in adapting a common form to an uncommon end.

CHAPTER V

SOME HISTORICAL PERSPECTIVES ON THE MONTEVERDI VESPERS

It is one of the paradoxes of musicological research that we generally become acquainted with a period, a repertoire, or a style through recognized masterworks that are tacitly or expressly assumed to be representative. Yet a masterpiece, by definition, is unrepresentative, unusual, and beyond the scope of ordinary musical activity. A more thorough and realistic knowledge of music history must come from a broader and deeper acquaintance with its constituent elements than is provided by a limited quantity of exceptional composers and works.

Such an expansion of the range of our historical research has the advantage not only of enhancing our understanding of a given topic, but also of supplying the basis for comparison among those works and artists who have faded into obscurity and the few composers and masterpieces that have survived to become the primary focus of our attention today. Only in relation to lesser efforts can we fully comprehend the qualities that raise the masterpiece above the common level. Only by comparison can we learn to what degree the master composer has rooted his creation in contemporary currents, or conversely, to what extent original ideas and techniques are responsible for its special features. Similarly, it is only by means of broader investigations that we can detect what specific historical influence the masterwork has had upon contemporaries and younger colleagues, and thereby arrive at judgments about the historical significance of the master composer.

Despite the obvious importance of systematic comparative studies, our comprehension of many a masterpiece still derives mostly from the artifact itself, resulting inevitably in an incomplete and distorted perspective. An archetypical case in point is Claudio Monteverdi's *Vespro della Beata Vergine* of 1610, which has received widespread attention in recent years, but almost entirely as an isolated phenomenon.[1] This is hardly surprising in view of the fact that Vesper psalms and Magnificats of the seventeenth century have been the subject of very few scholarly studies, and the few-voiced motet repertoire of the early *Seicento* (there are four such motets in the Monteverdi Vespers) has scarcely fared better.[2]

As a result, studies of the Monteverdi Vespers have hardly begun to treat the major historical issues posed by the publication's relationship to contemporary and subsequent Vesper repertoire. Most research has focused instead upon the liturgical question raised by the alternation of psalms and *sacri concentus* throughout the original print.[3] But even this troublesome problem might be further illuminated by an investigation of contemporary Vesper music. It is through just such an examination of the historical context of the *Vespro della Beata Vergine* that a broadening of our perspectives on this important work will be attempted in this essay.

I

A survey of extant Vesper music prints from the late sixteenth and early seventeenth centuries reveals several different categories of publications. The main type of print in the late *Cinquecento* consists of single settings of psalms *"per tutte le solennità"* (the actual number may vary from thirteen to twenty-one), following the example established by Willaert and Jachet of Mantua in their celebrated collection of 1550.[4] These prints supply polyphonic psalms for all the major feasts of the liturgical year (excluding ferial Vespers), frequently incorporate one or more Magnificats, and sometimes begin with a polyphonic setting of the Vesper respond, *Domine ad adiuvandum*. *Falsibordoni* may also be included, and a few Vesper collections after 1589 contain a single mass setting. Such publications form a rather homogeneous repertoire, each collection designed to fill the same liturgical needs.

Late in the sixteenth century, however, some new types of Vesper collections embracing a greater diversity of compositions began to appear alongside the old. In addition to Vesper psalms for all the major feasts, a small number of motets was sometimes admitted; frequently the four Marian antiphons for Compline were included; and *falsibordoni* in all the tones were common. This diversity of contents became especially significant during the last decade of the century, confirming further the breakdown of traditional formulas and techniques often observed in music of this period.[5]

These complex collections could easily grow to unwieldy proportions. By the time a composer assembled a complete Mass Ordinary, settings of all the Vesper psalms, some five or six motets, two or three Magnificats, *falsibordoni,* and perhaps even four Marian antiphons, his publication had become inordinately large and correspondingly expensive.[6] The practical response to this problem was to reduce the number of psalm settings, leaving just enough to cover most efficiently the largest possible number of feasts. A collection first published in 1599 by Antonio Mortaro of Milan illustrates this solution.[7] Mortaro's print contains a parody mass, the Vesper respond, the psalms *Dixit Dominus, Laudate pueri, Laetatus sum, Nisi Dominus, Lauda Ierusalem, Confitebor tibi, Beatus vir,* and *Laudate Dominum,* four motets, two *Magnificats* (one a parody Magnificat), and a set of *falsibordoni.* The eight psalms represent a substantial reduction in the number of psalm settings, but they are carefully chosen. The first five are those required for all Marian feasts and feasts of other virgins as indicated in the Common of the Saints. The last three, in conjunction with *Dixit Dominus* and *Laudate pueri,* serve for a variety of feasts from the Common, including first Vespers for feasts of Apostles and Evangelists, Confessor Bishops, One or Several Martyrs, and One or Several Pontiffs. The first group of psalms may be characterized as the "female *cursus*" and the second as the "male *cursus*."[8] These eight psalms, therefore, while not covering the entire liturgical year, could still prove quite useful to any choirmaster.

In fact, Mortaro's entire collection is designed with a multiplicity of practical purposes in mind. The mass setting, of course, is part of a completely separate rite which preceded Vespers during the day. The motets might have been employed in a variety of ways: possibly during the performance of the mass, perhaps in the Vesper service, in church on other occasions when their texts were suitable, or even in secular surroundings. The *Magnificats* are part of the Vesper Ordinary, and the textless *falsibordoni* provide alternative possibilities for singing the psalms (including all those omitted from the collection). They could even have been used for ferial Vespers or other services requiring psalms, such as Compline.

Not only does Mortaro's collection possess considerable flexibility in its practical application, but it also furnishes a more complete body of music for a single Vesper service than the collections *"per tutte le solennità."* In the one publication a *maestro di cappella* had enough music to perform an elaborate polyphonic Mass and Vespers on an appropriate feast day. Not only are all the major items supplied, but there is also a polyphonic setting of the respond and several motets from which to choose.

Mortaro's collection is illustrative of several related tendencies in sacred music publications around the turn of the seventeenth century. First, the contents affirm the aforementioned breakdown of the homogeneous collection. Second, this breakdown reveals a desire for more flexible practical applications of the single publication. And third, the provision of enough music for an elaborate polyphonic service reflects an interest in expanding the scope of polyphony at Vespers. That all three are broad-based historical trends is demonstrated by the fact that during the period 1600-1610 such complex publications, often with widely varying contents, more than tripled in quantity in comparison to the last decade of the sixteenth century.

The reduction in the number of psalm settings in a single collection is occasionally carried a step further than in Mortaro's print of 1599. A comparatively small number of publications survive that include only five Vesper psalms, placing even further limitations on the collection's use during the liturgical year. The earliest extant print restricted to just five psalms is a large and complex compilation by Diego Ortiz dating from 1565.[9] This publication contains a large number of hymns, a *Magnificat* in each of the eight tones, music from Compline, thirteen motets (mostly Marian antiphons), and the five Vesper psalms comprising the "male *cursus*." Ortiz's collection appears to be the first of such complexity and with such a multiplicity of purposes. It anticipates by a quarter century any significant trends in these directions. What is of particular interest, however, is the inclusion of psalms for only a few specific categories of feasts, a situation anticipating Monteverdi's own Vespers by forty-five years.

A 1590 publication for double choir by Orfeo Vecchi of Milan likewise contains only five psalms, though the remainder of the collection is more comparable to the 1599 print of Vecchi's Milanese colleague, Mortaro.[10] The five psalms in Vecchi's print, *Dixit Dominus, Confitebor tibi, Beatus vir, Laudate pueri,* and *In exitu Israel,* form the series for Sunday Vespers as indicated on the title page. Vecchi also includes a single mass, a setting of the Vesper respond, a *Magnificat*, three motets, and *falsibordoni.* Vecchi's collection does not lend itself to as many uses as Mortaro's, but like his, it contains enough music for an elaborate polyphonic Mass and Vespers, this time limited to Sundays. The function of the three motets is not entirely clear; in fact, they are not even listed in the title of the publication. Evidently, they may be inserted into the mass or Vesper service as desired. The *falsibordoni,* on the other hand, could serve the variety of functions cited above in connection with the *falsibordoni* of the Mortaro print.

After the turn of the seventeenth century, publications like those of Mortaro and Vecchi increased in number. I have been able to locate some sixteen collections from between 1600 and 1620 that limit their psalms to either the "male *cursus*" or the "female *cursus*," the latter holding the numerical edge with ten.[11] Several of those with the "female *cursus*" (including Monteverdi's) are specified on the title page as pertaining to feasts of the Virgin Mary, though, as mentioned earlier, they would also be suitable for feasts of other virgin saints. But the inclusion of the five Marian Vesper psalms is not the only ground for comparison between some of these collections and Monteverdi's Vespers. In several, the remaining contents are also similar, though nowhere identical.

Monteverdi's collection begins with the famous parody mass *In illo tempore,* which is then succeeded by the Vesper respond, *Domine ad adiuvandum.* Next comes a regular alternation between the five psalms and five *sacri concentus,* followed by the hymn *Ave maris stella* and two *Magnificats.*[12] A 1601 collection by Francesco Terriera is similar but a little smaller in dimensions.[13] A single mass is succeeded by the five Marian Vesper psalms, one *Magnificat,* and four motets. A 1606 print by Don Serafino Patta is somewhat more expansive, with the Vesper respond inserted between the mass and the first psalm, *falsibordoni* added after the *Magnificat,* the motets increased to five, and a setting of the Litany of the B.V.M. appended at the end. Ioannis Righi's publication from the same year is very similar.[14] The contents follow the same pattern as Patta's, but Righi adds a second *Magnificat,* includes only four motets, and places the Litany and *falsibordoni* last. In 1608, Pompeo Signorucci positioned a mass at the conclusion of his print, added a sixth psalm, *Laudate Dominum,* and incorporated three motets, but did not supply a Litany or *falsibordoni.*[15]

These are the only Marian Vesper collections antedating Monteverdi's that I have been able to find. The main differences between Monteverdi's and the others are his interspersal of the motets *between* the psalms, his inclusion of the Marian Vesper hymn, and his omission of anything else not directly connected with the Mass or Vespers, such as the Litany. It is the first of these differences that has given rise to so much controversy over the collection. It has been argued on the one hand that the motets are extraneous to the Vesper service, and on the other that they serve as substitutes for the plainchant antiphons normally required by the liturgy, a function indicated by their position between the psalms in the original print.[16]

The most recent and persuasive evidence has been gathered on the side of the antiphon-substitute theory, but even these arguments have taken limited cognizance of the evidence supplied by comparable contemporaneous collections.[17] The question why motets were included in Monteverdi's publication if they were not to be used in the Vesper service can also be asked about the other prints just listed, even if the motets come only at the end of each part-book. If these Marian Vesper collections, in contrast to those *"per tutte le solennità"* and those with multiple functions, were designed to provide a greater quantity of polyphonic music for a single category of feast, the reasonable assumption is that the few motets included are also usable as part of the liturgical performance.

More direct evidence of antiphon substitutes is found in a 1619 publication by the Roman composer Paolo Agostini.[18] The succession of works in this print is as follows:

> *Dixit Dominus,* secondo tono
> *Dum esset Rex,* antifona prima
> *Dixit Dominus,* primo tono
> *Sub tuum praesidium*
> *Laudate pueri,* sesto tono
> *Leva eius,* seconda antifona

Laudate pueri, intonatione del sesto tono
Virgo prudentissima
Laudate pueri, intonatione del quarto tono
Beata es Virgo
Laetatus sum, sesto tono
Nigra sum, tertia antifona
Laetatus sum, quarto tono
Cantate Domino
Nisi Dominus, secondo tono
Iam hiems transiit, antifona quarta
Nisi Dominus, ottavo tono
Veni in hortum meum
Lauda Hierusalem, ottavo tono
Speciosa facta es, quinta e ultima antifona
Lauda Hierusalem, primo tono
Gaudeamus omnes
Ave Maris Stella
Ave Maris Stella
Magnificat, ottavo tono
Beata Mater, antifona ad Magnificat
Magnificat, secondo tono
Ego dormio
Magnificat, secondo tono
Ab initio
Veni de Libano

The table of contents at the end of each part-book actually obscures this order. Instead of following the succession of pieces, the index groups all compositions in a single genre together, with the motets and antiphons for one, two, and three voices following after the psalms, hymns, and *Magnificat*s.

Agostini's collection is another of those devoted exclusively to Vespers of the Virgin, but it differs from all earlier examples in presenting multiple settings of each of the psalms. It is also the only collection besides Monteverdi's to include the hymn *Ave maris stella* (in two settings), but most importantly, Agostini follows Monteverdi's precedent in interspersing the antiphons and motets between the psalms. His method is systematic and clearly indicates the liturgical function of the motets. Each psalm in the collection has two settings, except *Laudate pueri,* which has three. The first version of a psalm is followed by a polyphonic composition on the appropriate antiphon text for Marian feasts from the Common of the Saints. These pieces are labelled *"antifona prima," "antifona seconda,"* etc. However, these antiphon texts are not suitable for *all* Marian feasts. Those feasts listed in the Proper of the Time require their own antiphons. Agostini resolves the problem of the proliferation of antiphons by furnishing single substitute texts, set polyphonically and placed after the second (and third in the case of *Laudate pueri*) version of each psalm in the print. Thus every motet occupies the same position relative to the preceding psalm as does each of the polyphonic antiphon settings derived from the Common of the Saints. There seems to be no alternative but to accept these motets as antiphon-substitutes for use in Marian feasts from the Proper of the Time. The analogy with Monteverdi's collection is obvious and offers further support for performing his *sacri concentus* in place of plainchant antiphons.

Stephen Bonta, arguing in favor of the antiphon-substitute theory, notes that it is impossible to find in the *Liber Usualis* liturgically correct plainchant antiphons that fit the tonalities of Monteverdi's five psalms.[19] The same observation may be made with regard to all the collections of Marian Vespers published between 1600 and 1620. In none of these does the succession of psalm tonalities match the *Liber's* modes for plainchant antiphons from the Common of the Saints or from any Marian feast in the Proper. This difficulty, which Bonta suggests was resolved by substituting polyphonic motets that did not have to agree with the psalm in tonality, has implications extending beyond Monteverdi's own Vespers and the Marian Vespers of other composers.

The fact is that any polyphonic setting of a Vesper psalm necessitated a choice of a single tonality, thereby limiting the number of modally compatible plainchant antiphons with which the psalm could be sung. Since it is the *antiphon* that is proper to a particular feast day or group of feasts (as in the Common), the ability of the psalm to match the mode of the antiphon was crucial to whether or not the psalm could be used for a particular feast. Thus a polyphonic psalm composition would be limited to fewer feasts than its Gregorian counterpart. Presumably it could only be sung when the plainchant antiphon happened to be in the same mode.

One of the earliest means of circumventing this dilemma, initially engendered by the desire for polyphonic music at Vespers, was to supply *falsibordoni* psalms in all the tones. These chordal harmonizations of the psalm chant, typically with an additional melisma appended at the mediant and end, were normally textless and most often appeared in manuscripts and prints in all tones. Thus any psalm text could be fitted to a *falsobordone* in whatever tone was required.

Once a specific psalm text was set in *canto figurato,* however, this flexibility was lost and the tonality was fixed. Thus a question is raised about the practical use of polyphonic Vesper psalms, which began appearing with some frequency in manuscripts of the first half of the sixteenth century, increasing greatly in number after the early publications of the 1550s. It seems that the possibilities for using a given psalm in a fixed tonality would have been rather limited. The problem is further complicated by an examination of the tones of polyphonic settings as designated in the indices of a good many sixteenth-century prints. Frequently a Vesper collection begins with the psalms *Dixit Dominus, Confitebor tibi, Beatus vir,* and *Laudate pueri* (Psalms 109, 110, 111, and 112). Traditionally, these four psalms were in the first four tones, though at times other tones were also indicated. This custom even antedates the earliest published Vesper psalms, being traceable in manuscripts as far back as the late fifteenth century.[20]

But if one examines the *Liber Usualis* for the most common modes of antiphons for these four psalms, major discrepancies are revealed. Antiphons for *Dixit Dominus* most frequently fall in the eighth mode and to a lesser extent in the seventh. Antiphons for *Confitebor tibi* and *Laudate pueri* are likewise most often in the seventh and eighth modes. Similarly, the majority of *Beatus vir* antiphons are in the eighth mode, although a lesser number are distributed fairly evenly among the first, fourth, and seventh modes. Thus the first four Vesper psalms were normally not even set in the most common modes of their antiphons, at least as far as the *Liber Usualis* is concerned. Here, however, we must call into question the accuracy with which modern liturgical books represent sixteenth- and seventeenth-century liturgical conditions. Though the Church was constantly pressing for a more unified liturgy after the Council of Trent (1545-1563), there still remain many divergences between the practices manifested in publications of the period and those standardized in modern books.[21]

For example, some of the psalm intonations given in collections of Vesper music do not match any found in the *Liber Usualis*. Other discrepancies emerge from Adriano Banchieri's *L'Organo Suonarino* of 1605.[22] In the *Secondo registro,* Banchieri supplies organ basses to be alternated with chant for eight psalms, each in one of the eight tones. Feasts for which these psalms are proper are listed at the head of each. But in several cases the feasts named call for antiphons that in the *Liber* are in different modes from Banchieri's psalms. For instance, Banchieri's setting of *Laetatus sum* in the sixth tone is specified as appropriate to the Marian feasts of the Nativity, Visitation, Conception, and Presentation.[23] But the *Liber* has sixth mode antiphons for this psalm only for the feast of the Nativity of the Virgin. For the other feasts listed by Banchieri, the *Liber* calls for the third, eighth, and third modes respectively. Similar disparities are posed by the rubrics of two more of Banchieri's organ basses.[24]

The larger question, how polyphonic psalm settings were used during this period and what their relationship to plainchant antiphons actually was, is still in need of clarification. As Bonta suggests, it is quite likely that the problem of matching a Gregorian antiphon to a polyphonic psalm (most often beginning with a plainchant intonation) was frequently sidestepped by the substitution of a polyphonic motet for the proper antiphon.[25] This appears to have been Monteverdi's solution as well as that of Agostini and some of the other composers of Marian Vespers mentioned above. James Armstrong's study of the Anerio *Antiphonae* reinforces this view.

It is worth re-emphasizing that even though the antiphon-substitute theory appears valid, Monteverdi, more than the authors of most such collections, stresses the flexible uses of the motets and other music of his publication.[26] Yet his title page, which suggests that the *sacri concentus* (and perhaps other items) could be performed outside the church and apart from a liturgical service, has contributed to the confusion of modern scholars over his intentions. It is even possible that the ambiguity of the title was deliberate. Monteverdi's designation of at least part of the contents as *"ad Sacella sive Principum Cubicula accommodata,"* "suitable for chapels or the chambers of princes," may have been intended not only to suggest optional uses for various pieces in the collection, but also to veil the role of the *sacri concentus* as possible antiphon-substitutes from the casual observer, such as an ecclesiastical censor. Substitutions were outside officially sanctioned liturgical practice, and it must be recalled that the Mass and Vespers were dedicated to Pope Paul V. The only complete table of contents is in the organ *partitura* and one would have had to look there to realize the liturgical role the *sacri concentus* could play. Such a mild deception may also have been the reason behind Agostini's listing of antiphons and motets *after* the psalms, hymns, and *Magnificat*s in the index of his 1619 Marian Vespers rather than in their actual order of appearance in the part-books. Twentieth-century controversies over the liturgical use of these motets ironically may bear witness to the success of such a ploy.

II

The musical aspects of the *Vespro della Beata Vergine* present a complex picture, both in their own right and in comparison with the contemporaneous Vesper repertoire. Just as it proved necessary to examine the historical background of Vesper collections in order to obtain a perspective on the contents and organization of Monteverdi's print, it is equally essential to investigate the compositional techniques and styles of Vesper music, both before and after 1610, to understand the relationship between Monteverdi's work and the efforts of others.

A few general points of reference may be established at the outset. First, Monteverdi's seems to be the earliest Vesper publication requiring *obbligato* instruments. The use of instruments to double or replace vocal lines *ad libitum* had been suggested on the title pages of many sixteenth-century motet collections, and *obbligato* instrumental parts appear in a few early *Seicento* motet books. But in the Vesper repertoire I have found no prior examples of *obbligato* orchestration, and even Monteverdi's optional instrumentation has very few precedents.[27]

A second peculiarity of Monteverdi's collection is the extensive employment of a *cantus firmus* in the psalms and *Magnificats*. While *cantus firmi* do appear sporadically in Vesper music, as demonstrated below, they are nowhere as ubiquitous as in Monteverdi's print of 1610.

Third, all of the music of the *Vespro* is composed in an elaborate style. This is true not only with regard to the virtuoso character of much of the vocal and instrumental writing, but also with respect to Monteverdi's large-scale, complicated structures. The psalms and *Magnificats* are more expansive and possess more internal stylistic contrasts than any previous examples. The motets are musically more sophisticated than most such contemporary pieces, and *Duo Seraphim* exhibits more virtuoso embellishment than any other motet from the early *Seicento* I have seen. The *Sonata sopra Sancta Maria* is ampler in both size and sonority than the several models on which it is based. Even the respond and hymn are larger and more grandiose than the settings of other composers. Consistent with such complexity and diversity, Monteverdi's is the only collection of Vesper music up to this time to vary the number of voices required from one piece to the next.

In sum, we may begin with the general observation that the Monteverdi Vespers are on an unparalleled level of musical splendor in the exploitation of vocal and instrumental colors and virtuosity, in the complexity of structures and textures, in the variety of styles and techniques, and in the magnitude of individual pieces. This musical opulence may be traced to a number of sources: Monteverdi's obvious desire to establish himself through this one collection as an eminent composer of sacred music in both the old style (the *Missa In illo tempore*) and almost every new style then in the process of development; the possible origin of at least part of the Vespers as music for a lavish celebration in Mantua; or the personal taste of Duke Vincenzo Gonzaga, reflected in the designation on the title page *"ad Sacella sive Principum Cubicula accommodata,"* which suggests the duke's private chapel and rooms in contrast to *"ad Ecclesiam,"* a public church.[28] Whatever the genesis of the stylistic idiosyncrasies of the Vespers, our *historical* perspective can be enhanced only by an examination of the precedents upon which Monteverdi has expanded and an investigation of the impact of his novel approach to Vesper music in the period immediately following his publication of the work in 1610.

The Vesper psalm repertoire of the first decade of the seventeenth century is an extension of the styles and techniques of the late *Cinquecento*. The revolution in secular music and the motet, already in progress around the turn of the century, had had by 1610 only a limited effect on polyphonic psalmody. In one sense this is paradoxical, for psalm settings, which had always relied heavily on a chordal style originating in harmonization of the psalm tone, were by their very nature closer to the newly evolved concepts of homophony and intelligible declamation than were many other forms of sixteenth-century music. In addition, the verse structure of psalm texts automatically divided a composition into discrete sections, both in *alternatim* and through-composed settings. Such sectionalization of large compositions into smaller components, often contrasting in texture, meter, or style, was another of the characteristic developments of the early *Seicento*.

But opposing those aspects of polyphonic psalmody that were compatible with modern trends was the conservative aesthetic view of this liturgical genre, exemplified by the brief remarks of Pietro Cerone in 1613:

> In composing psalms, even to omit imitating the psalmody will be no error, for if one were to imitate the plainsong in all the parts, repeating the motives, the verse would be very long, very elaborate, and overly solemn, solemnity being unsuited to psalmody. . . . Be it further observed that the music should be such as does not obscure the words, which should be very distinct and clear, so that all the parts will seem to enunciate together, no more, no less, as in a falso bordone, without long or elegant passages or any novelty other than ordinary consonances, introducing from time to time some short and commonplace imitation. . . . To conclude, I say that any invention used in the verses of the psalms should be very short, formed of few notes and these of small value, and also that the parts should enter in succession after rests of not more than one, two, three, or sometimes four measures. And this should be observed both to avoid making the verses long and to avoid falling into the style of the three privileged canticles.[29]

Although Cerone reproaches Italian composers for sometimes violating the simplicity of psalmody, his aesthetic orientation is corroborated by countless psalm collections of the time. Whether completely homophonic or incorporating polyphonic imitation, whether set for a single choir or *cori spezzati,* Vesper psalms were not the place for a composer to display his prowess, nor were they considered suitable for instrumental doubling after the fashion of masses and motets. Psalms were more purely functional than decorative. They tended to be unpretentious and lacking in the artifice and solemnity bestowed on masses, motets, and even Magnificats. In many respects, Vesper psalmody represented the ideal type of liturgical music when measured against the precepts of the Council of Trent. The clearly declaimed homophony of psalm settings matched perfectly the Council's requirements for sacred music, though the reformers' main concern was the mass.[30]

Despite the conservative tendencies of Vesper psalmody, a few impulses in the direction of modernity can be witnessed in the first decade of the seventeenth century. The natural subdivision of a psalm into several sections invited contrasts among those sections, and composers in the early *Seicento* gradually began to take advantage of such opportunities. A 1601 through-composed setting of *Nisi Dominus* by Monteverdi's Mantuan colleague, Giovanni Giacomo Gastoldi, not only utilizes antiphonal,

EXAMPLE 1. Giovanni GASTOLDI, *Nisi Dominus*

homophonic four-voice choirs in duple time, but also shifts to triple meter three times in the course of the piece and includes a passage of *falsobordone* as well.[31] The block-like exchanges between the two choirs, frequently comprising entire lines of text (see example 1), denote a forerunner of Monteverdi's own *Nisi Dominus,* though the latter work employs a plain-chant *cantus firmus* throughout and is considerably longer with its second choir echoing precisely each line sung by the first. Monteverdi's rhythms are also more varied than Gastoldi's and his part-writing is more complex, even though *Nisi Dominus* is the simplest and least progressive of the five psalms of the *Vespro.*[32] This type of antiphonal setting is common in the Vesper repertoire, though the dimensions of Monteverdi's version are typically larger.

Contrasting sections within a psalm are more fully exploited by Gastoldi in his 1607 six-voice setting of *Memento Domine David.*[33] This lengthy text requires considerable variety of treatment in order to maintain musical interest. Gastoldi employs homophonic textures for all six voices, chordal antiphony between the upper three and the lower three, polyphony in varying combinations of parts, *falsibordoni* followed by polyphonic melismas, sections in triple meter, and passages in faster note values than the prevailing rhythms. This may well be the most complex and varied psalm setting before 1610, but the styles of its component parts are rooted in the past and not comparable to the modern aspects of Monteverdi's even more complex psalms.

Composers outside the Mantuan circle also occasionally contrasted successive sections of a psalm, and there even survive a few compositions from before 1610 with emphasis partly or entirely on ornamented solo voices and the newest vocal styles. Both features are combined with *falsobordone* in a three-voice *Dixit Dominus* published in 1606 by Leone Leoni, employed at the time in Vicenza.[34] Leoni's *Dixit* contrasts the polyphonic texture of its first and last segments with internal sections of unmeasured recitation for one, two, and three voices.[35] The ornamental element consists of melismas following each half-verse in *falsobordone.* The melodic shapes and rhythmic patterns of these melismas are similar to much of the vocal writing in few-voiced motets from Viadana onward. They are not yet in the faster sixteenth notes favored by Monteverdi (see example 2).

Another example of the rather rare appearance of solo voices in psalm composition is found in Don Severo Bonini's Compline psalm, *Cum invocarem,* published in 1609.[36] This piece is an unabashed monody modeled on those of Bonini's Florentine compatriot Caccini, particularly in the extensive use of the most modern ornaments. As in Leoni's *Dixit Dominus,* the ornamental passages follow the initial part of each line, which is set in *falsobordone* (see example 3).

EXAMPLE 2. Leone LEONI, *Dixit Dominus*

EXAMPLE 3. Don Severo BONINI, *Cum invocarem*

It is significant that both the Leoni and Bonini psalms were not printed in collections of Vesper music, but in books of motets (madrigals and motets in the case of Bonini). The inclusion of occasional Vesper psalms in motet books seems to have led to the assimilation by these psalms of the style of their companion pieces. It is actually in this peripheral part of the psalm repertoire that we find the forerunners of the few-voiced sections of Monteverdi's *Dixit Dominus, Laudate pueri,* and *Laetatus sum.* Monteverdi's is thus the first publication of Vesper music to amalgamate the full-choir techniques common to psalmody with the newer few-voiced virtuoso style.

Many of the precedents for Monteverdi's separate *obbligato* and optional instrumental parts in the Vespers also derive from the motet repertoire.[37] A book of *Concerti Ecclesiastici* published in 1608 by Arcangelo Crotti of Ferrara includes several pieces for one or two soloists with notated instrumental accompaniments, most of which are marked *si placet.*[38] In Caterina Assandra's motet collection of 1609, one piece, *O salutaris Hostia,* is set for soprano and bass supported by a violin and *violone* in addition to the basso continuo.[39]

The most famous example of *obbligato* instrumentation in motets, of course, is Giovanni Gabrieli's *Sacrae Symphoniae* of 1615.[40] Since Gabrieli died in 1612, the contents of this collection antedate its publication by at least three years and in some cases by many more, as determined from concordances.[41]

A few instances of the use of instruments in connection with Vesper music may also be noted. Giulio Radino Padovano's *Concerti per sonare et cantare* of 1607 contains a sixteen-voice, *coro spezzato Magnificat* with the rubrics *"Choro de Violini, Choro de Cornetti, Choro de Tromboni,"* and *"Capella"* in various part-books.[42] The ensembles of instruments in this *Magnificat* seem perfectly natural in a collection devoted primarily to wholly instrumental music. One of the psalms in Agostino Agazzari's *Psalmi Sex* of 1609 is headed by the direction: *"Prima si fa una Sinfonia di stromenti,"* though this must be improvised because no music is given.[43] Denis Arnold describes a *Laudate pueri* by the Venetian Giovanni Croce, who died in 1609, in which one of three four-part choirs consists of a tenor and three instruments, "two of which are specified to be trombones."[44] The date of this piece is unknown, since its first appearance is in an anthology published in 1630.[45]

That *notated* instrumental parts became significant in sacred music at Mantua at about this time is evident not only from Monteverdi's Vespers, but also from Amante Franzoni's *Apparato Musicale* of 1613.[46] The Mass in this collection, which according to the preface was performed in the Ducal Church on the feast of Santa Barbara, contains an instrumental *En-*

trata in place of the Introit, an instrumental *ritornello* to be fitted between the segments of the *Kyrie,* a *canzona francese* to accompany the Epistle, *sinfonie* to be inserted between sections of the Offertory, two more *sinfonie* to precede the *Sanctus* and *Agnus,* and a *canzona* to conclude the service. As indicated on the title page, these instrumental pieces could be omitted, and they are not integral elements in any of the mass sections.[47]

The pervasive diffusion of the plainchant *cantus firmus* throughout the psalms and *Magnificat*s of the *Vespro della Beata Vergine* has been cited by Denis Arnold as evidence of Monteverdi's concern for structural cohesion in these expansive and variegated compositions.[48] But the monotony of the psalm tone also poses difficult aesthetic and organizational problems, as can be observed in the few other settings of the late sixteenth and early seventeenth centuries that rely heavily on the plainchant. While harmonization of the psalm tone had been practiced with some frequency in the early part of the *Cinquecento*, by late in the century most composers employed the *cantus firmus* sparingly. The reason is obvious: harmonic and tonal tedium are the almost inevitable result. One has only to look at some of the rare instances where the chant *was* used extensively. Victoria's *Dixit Dominus*, published in 1581, illustrates the harmonic limitations resulting therefrom.[49] The effect is much worse in Giovanni Croce's eight-voice, double-choir *Domine probasti me* of 1603.[50] This particular psalm text is of unusual length, and the desire to unify the composition is probably what prompted Croce to employ the chant in the first place. But even though the primary texture is relieved by several two-voice sections in the middle of the piece, the monotony of Croce's setting is almost overwhelming.

Most composers pay rather limited attention to the psalm tone if they use it at all. In the numerous psalms beginning with a plainchant intonation, the chant often continues in the tenor or soprano once the polyphony starts. Almost invariably, however, the psalm tone is abandoned after the completion of the first verse of the text. Similar treatment may be accorded interior sections of *alternatim* settings. Here too the plainchant begun in an even or odd verse may continue in one voice in the succeeding polyphonic segment. But this procedure rarely occurs in more than one or two sections in psalms of the late sixteenth or early seventeenth centuries.[51]

Aside from the continuation of the plainchant into a polyphonic texture, the psalm tone may also be confined entirely within a polyphonic segment itself. Most often this takes the form of single verses cast in unmeasured *falsibordoni*. In other instances the method may be harmonization in *canto figurato*. Occasionally the psalm tone appears as a long-note *cantus firmus*, serves as an imitative subject, or is even treated in canon.[52]

Such sophisticated contrapuntal procedures are exceptional and normally are found in only a single section of a composition. Whatever technique may be chosen, it is usually an isolated special occurrence within the polyphonic piece as a whole. Except for the Croce psalm mentioned above | and a work by Giovanni Francesco Capello to be discussed below, Monteverdi seems to be the only composer in the early seventeenth century to use the *cantus firmus* as a pervasive organizational device. It is a tribute to his imagination and genius that he was able to achieve both the desired structural cohesion and the harmonic, tonal, textural, and stylistic variety necessary to avoid the monotony that would otherwise have resulted.

The first stage in Monteverdi's compositional process throughout the Vespers consisted of the selection of relatively simple techniques and formal concepts derived from a variety of traditional and modern sources. These diverse materials were then combined in a new synthesis to forge large-scale, elaborate structures whose size and impact far surpass the creations of other composers. Nowhere is this more evident or striking than in the psalm *Dixit Dominus*. The symmetrical structure of this expansive setting may be seen in diagram II, p. 92.[53]

Structural symmetry was especially important to Monteverdi at this period in his life, as demonstrated by the Vespers and *L'Orfeo*, but the sequence of sections outlined in diagram 2 also represents a complex fusion of techniques practiced separately by other composers.[54] The opening imitative chorus employs as its main subject the psalm tone of the fourth mode. Such imitation based on the chant was nothing new, though ordinarily it can be found only in the most elaborate and sophisticated psalm settings. The passages of *falsibordoni*, commencing immediately after the opening, are quite common in Vesper psalmody, but Monteverdi's concluding melismas are more polyphonically elaborate than usual. Unique is the fact that each of these melismas is a rhythmic and melodic variant of a single basic harmonic pattern.[55] In addition, each of the optional instrumental *ritornelli* is a varied repetition of the immediately preceding melisma.

These *ritornelli* are without precedent in the Vesper repertoire. Their models may well have been the *ritornelli* of Monteverdi's own *L'Orfeo*, but as has been pointed out, separate instrumental parts were also gaining ground in sacred music at this time.

In *Dixit Dominus*, the section immediately following the first *ritornello* exhibits a modern style and texture based upon an old structural technique. Here a typical Baroque trio, consisting of two imitative voices in the same range supported by an independent bass part, makes its first appearance in Vesper psalmody. Similar trios are found in *Laudate pueri, Laetatus sum, Pulchra es, Duo Seraphim*, the *Sonata sopra Sancta Maria*, and both *Magnificats*. While such textures are common in Monteverdi's madrigals after 1600, they also occur frequently in the few-voiced motet books beginning with Viadana's *Cento Concerti Ecclesiastici* of 1602.[56] This underscores once again the influence of the motet repertoire on Monteverdi's collection.

What makes this passage in *Dixit Dominus* of particular interest is the character of the bass line. At first provided solely by the organ continuo, it is formed primarily from a single sustained chord. But as the second soprano enters in imitation of the first, a bass voice is also added, and the sustained chord in the organ proves to have been a simplification of the measured psalm-tone recitation in the bass. This same pattern of imitative upper voices supported by a psalm-tone bass recurs after the *ritornello* in each of the tripartite groups bracketed in diagram II. In the first two of these sections the old-fashioned technique of *falsobordone* serves as a foundation for the modern trio texture of the combined parts.

In the structure of *Dixit Dominus* as a whole, it is apparent that aside from the opening and closing polyphonic choruses, the remainder of the work is actually based on the extremely simple and traditional *alternatim* procedure whereby verses in *falsobordone* alternate with plainchant. But the *falsibordoni* are embellished by means of large polyphonic melismas and instrumental *ritornelli*, while the plainchant is rhythmicized and elaborated by the addition of imitative upper parts. The overall dimensions of the setting with its *falsibordoni*, *ritornelli*, trio textures, imitative choral polyphony, and extended six-voice melismas are so expansive as to obscure the humble origins of this very complex and splendid composition.

The remainder of the psalms in the *Vespro* also draw on a variety of both traditional and modern styles and techniques.[57] *Laudate pueri*, for example, embraces antiphonal writing, imitative polyphony, eight-voice homophony, virtuoso duets in counterpoint with the psalm tone, plainchant accompanied solely by the organ, and a concluding polyphonic melisma. *Laetatus sum*, on the other hand, is built on a series of varying textures unfolding over four separate bass patterns, which are themselves repeated in the sequence ABACD, ABACD, ABD. This complicated procedure has its roots in the strophic variations of *L'Orfeo* and the secular works of other early seventeenth-century composers, but is previously unknown in music for Vespers. *Nisi Dominus* bears a close relationship to antiphonal psalms by Gastoldi, as already described above. *Lauda Jerusalem* is reminiscent of *Nisi Dominus* in its greater consistency of texture and absence of few-voiced virtuoso passages. The seven parts form two three-voice choirs around the *cantus firmus* in the tenor, and the texture is both antiphonal and polyphonic with more rhythmic complexity and closer interaction between the vocal ensembles than in *Nisi Dominus*.

Thus the stylistic complexity and diversity witnessed in each individual psalm of the Vespers is reflected in the succession of pieces as well. The variety of sources from which Monteverdi has drawn and the constantly changing manner in which he has combined his materials is truly astonishing. Cohesion and diversity have been brought together in a dynamic synthesis that is one of the most significant factors in the aesthetic impact of these compositions.

The dialectical forces of cohesion and diversity also focus attention on the antithetical tendencies of conservatism and progressiveness. The pervasive *cantus firmus* is a thoroughly conservative device, no longer utilized by other composers of Vesper psalms. Monteverdi is fully conscious of this, for he openly advertises his approach to the psalm tone by inscribing in the basso continuo part-book the rubric "*composto sopra canti fermi.*" On the other hand, the old-fashioned *cantus firmus* is adorned in the several psalms with the most modern musical styles and textures, emphasizing contrast and heterogeneity, especially in the first three pieces. This dichotomy and tension between the old and the new is another fundamental aesthetic feature of these works.

While many detailed technical differences between Monteverdi's psalms and those of other composers may be cited, the larger issue of comparative aesthetic effect and the elements that create it is an equally important concern, though rather more elusive and difficult to verbalize. Monteverdi's psalms doubtless make a stronger impression on the listener than those of his colleagues. Although many factors contribute to this, there can be little question that among the most important are the dynamic tensions between cohesion and diversity, between conservatism and modernity described here.

In brief summary, Monteverdi's psalms are shaped from a variety of traditional techniques in combination with modern stylistic developments derived primarily from the motet repertoire. This fusion of diverse materials results in complex, expansive structures which are much more ornate, elaborate, and impressive than anything produced by either his predecessors or his contemporaries.

III

Monteverdi's two *Magnificat*s (one a close variation upon the other) are even more unusual in comparison with the repertoire of the late sixteenth and early seventeenth centuries than are his psalms.[58] The Canticle of Mary has a longer history of polyphonic composition than Vesper psalmody, and it was customarily treated in a more elaborate style.[59] Cerone emphasizes this relationship in his commentary on the three principal canticles:

> As is the custom, the three principal canticles, namely, the Magnificat, the Nunc dimittis, and the Benedictus Dominus Deus Israel, are always made solemn; for this reason, they must be composed in a more lofty style and with more art and more skill than the other canticles and the psalms.[60]

As in psalm settings, the importance of the plainchant *cantus firmus* in Magnificats gradually subsided as the sixteenth century progressed.

In Costanzo Festa's *Magnificats* from the 1530s, a paraphrase of the Magnificat tone serves as the subject for imitation at the beginning of almost every verse.[61] From time to time the *cantus firmus* surfaces in longer note values in a single part, usually the topmost. As the chant approaches its cadence, the tone is almost invariably ornamented. Most of Festa's *Magnificats* have at least one segment in which the Magnificat tone is treated in strict canon between two voices.

Similar techniques are employed in the *Magnificats* of Morales and Victoria, published in 1545 and 1576 respectively, although the Magnificat tone is not so omnipresent as in the works of Festa.[62] The plainchant is much less significant, however, in the *Magnificats* of Palestrina.[63] Palestrina rarely uses more than the *initium* of the chant melody, usually as the imitative subject of his polyphonic texture. In those instances where the chant does continue beyond the opening of a section, it is so highly embellished as to be virtually unrecognizable; the recitation tone appears only occasionally as a single pitch in an active, flowing line. Many sections of the Palestrina *Magnificats* show no evidence of the Magnificat tone whatsoever.

Interest in the Magnificat-tone *cantus firmus* continued to decline into the seventeenth century. *Alternatim* settings, of course, which constitute perhaps half of all Magnificats from the early *Seicento*, would still have every other verse sung in plainchant in the same manner as *alternatim* psalms. But printed Magnificats having any reference to the chant in their polyphonic verses comprise less than half the extant repertoire. Where a borrowed plainsong does occur, it is normally confined to the continuation of a solo intonation into the first part of the polyphonic setting, equivalent to the practice in psalmody. In some compositions the *initium* of the Magnificat tone opens a polyphonic segment other than the first, but rarely does the chant appear in more than one such section. The custom of setting the Doxology in canon based on the Magnificat tone survives only marginally.[64] By the time of Monteverdi's *Vespro*, only vestiges of the earlier significance of the Magnificat chant remain. The usages one meets in the early seventeenth century do not differ substantially from those encountered in psalmody.

The waning importance of the chant sets in striking relief Monteverdi's highly original approach to the *cantus firmus* in his two *Magnificats* of 1610. In his psalms Monteverdi usually gave to the *cantus firmus* rhythmic values commensurate with the other voices. As a result, even though the chant regulates the basic harmony, the tone itself is often absorbed into the larger texture. In the *Magnificats*, however, the chant is set in long notes and stands apart from the other voices and instruments. This type of strict, long-note *cantus firmus* has no precedent in the history of the Marian canticle. Monteverdi ignored the traditions of this repertoire and revived instead the oldest *cantus firmus* technique of the mass, applying it to his *Magnificat*s with great rigor.

The result is a continuous series of variations on the Magnificat tone, with the other parts disporting themselves in the most progressive styles.[65] Once again the multiplicity and diversity of Monteverdi's sources is revealed, and once again the virtuosity with which they are combined is astounding.

Monteverdi's utilization of modern techniques is more pronounced in the canticles than in the psalms. With the exception of choral textures in the first and last verses of the seven-voice *Magnificat* and in the first and final two verses of the six-voice setting, the remaining sections are devoted to solo writing, trio textures, vocal and instrumental virtuosity, dialogues, echo duets, *ritornello* structures, *obbligato* instrumental accompaniments, and rapid note values; in short, a dazzling array of the most recently developed styles and structures, all unified by the severe and unremitting presence of the *cantus firmus*. The tension between diversity and cohesion, between modernity and conservatism, is even more starkly evident here than in the psalms.

Though one may search vainly in the early seventeenth-century sacred repertoire for anything comparable, adumbrations of a few of Monteverdi's techniques do appear between 1600 and 1610. In this decade contrasts in sonority, texture, and style among successive sections began to emerge in Magnificats as they did in Vesper psalms. Variations in sonority assume importance in an *alternatim Magnificat* from Viadana's *Cento Concerti Ecclesiastici* of 1602. While the polyphonic texture remains three-voiced throughout, the combination of voices changes at several stages along the way. Initially the trio comprises soprano, alto, and bass, but the parts shift to soprano and two altos at the *Et misericordia*; alto, tenor, and bass at the *Deposuit*; soprano, alto, and tenor at *Suscepit Israel*; and then return to the original voicing for the *Gloria Patri*. There are no changes in style in the course of the piece, however, aside from a short passage of *falsobordone* in the *Deposuit*.

Contrasts in style are manifest in a five-voice *alternatim Magnificat* by Gastoldi, also published in 1602.[66] Most of the piece is conceived in imitative polyphony, but the *Deposuit* is set in *falsobordone*, the *Et misericordia* employs a reduced number of voices (a long-standing tradition in Magnificat composition), and the Doxology deviates to triple meter.

Even greater contrasts may be observed in a four-voice *alternatim Magnificat* by Leone Leoni from 1606.[67] The traditional reduction in number of voices is retained in the *Fecit potentiam* and the *Esurientes*, but

EXAMPLE 4. Leone LEONI, *Magnificat*

the resulting duets for soprano and tenor, alto and bass, display a more embellished vocal line than the four-voice sections (see example 4). The other segments rely heavily on *falsibordoni* followed by polyphonic textures, which are sometimes melismatic. There is even a sequential imitative passage very similar to the polyphonic melismas of Monteverdi's *Dixit Dominus* (see example 5).

EXAMPLE 5. Leone LEONI, *Magnificat*

Trio textures and virtuoso solo writing are prominent in a 1607 *alternatim Magnificat* by Tiburtio Massaino, who, like Monteverdi, was in the employ of the Duke of Mantua.[68] In this setting for two voices and organ continuo (the organ part-book is missing from the British Museum copy), Massaino writes particularly elaborate parts, amply endowed with ornaments in small note values and modern dotted rhythms. Massaino adheres to custom by reducing the number of voices for two interior sections, but the outcome is a very untraditional florid monody. The duet passages are consistently imitative, and the parts frequently proceed in parallel thirds and sixths after an initial point of imitation, a favorite device of Monteverdi's (see example 6).

The last few years of the first decade of the century witnessed mounting interest in virtuoso writing in Magnificats. Giovanni Luca Conforti's *Passaggi sopra tutti li salmi* of 1607 applies diminutions, often reaching extraordinary proportions, to his *Magnificat* as well as his psalms (see example 7).[69] The two *Magnificat*s in Ottavio Durante's *Arie Devote* of 1608 are also prolific in their ornamentation, but the embellishments are conceived as an integral part of the melodic line (see example 8).[70]

Significantly, all of the few-voiced, virtuoso Magnificat settings

EXAMPLE 6. Tiburtio MASSAINO, *Magnificat*

described here, with the exception of Conforti's, were published in motet books rather than Vesper collections. While Vesper psalms appeared only rarely outside prints devoted specifically to Vesper music (cf. the Leoni and Bonini examples discussed above), Magnificats are found not only in psalm and Magnificat publications, but also in books of *mottetti, concerti ecclesiastici, sacri concentus*, etc. As a result, several types of Magnificat developed in the early seventeenth century. Those canticles incorporated into Vesper collections tended to be similar to the psalms with which they were printed, whether the style was homophonic, imitative, or *coro spezzato*. Magnificats in motet books likewise corresponded to the style of the pieces they accompanied. Since the motet was the genre in which few-voiced writing first penetrated into sacred music in the early *Seicento*, Magnificats frequently assumed the new textures by association. As virtuoso embellishments invaded the motet repertoire around 1604, increasing in intensity during the next several years, Magnificats were also affected, as illustrated by those of Massaino and Durante.

These observations demonstrate that in composing his canticles Monteverdi once again took the motet books rather than contemporary Vesper collections as his point of departure. It is in the motet repertoire that one finds the precedents for his few-voiced virtuoso writing in the *Magnificat*s and the psalms, even though the inventory of pieces in the *Vespro della Beata Vergine* is modeled on the other Marian Vesper publications described in part I of this essay.

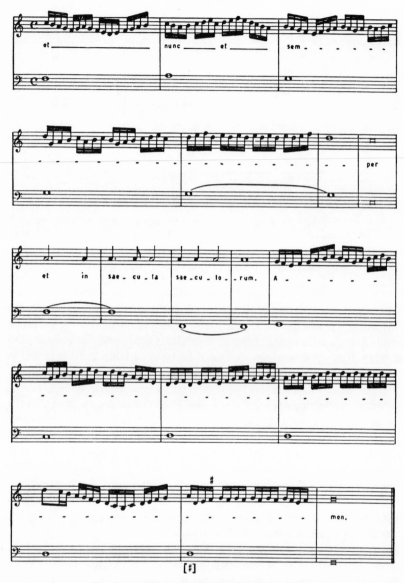

EXAMPLE 7. Luca CONFORTI, *Magnificat*

EXAMPLE 8. Ottavio DURANTE, *Magnificat*

Despite the foreshadowing of a few of Monteverdi's techniques in several early seventeenth-century motet books, his *Magnificat*s emerge as even more original expressions of his artistic genius than his psalms. The dialectical synthesis of modern styles and an antiquated form of the *cantus firmus*, the expansive dimensions of both settings, and the extensive use of *obbligato* instruments in the *Magnificat à 7* are all unparalleled in the previous history of the Marian canticle. While Monteverdi's psalms employ both traditional and contemporary styles and devices in new and original combinations, his unique *Magnificat*s exhibit only minimal connections with the remainder of the repertoire.

IV

The *sacri concentus* of the *Vespro della Beata Vergine* comprise the celebrated *Sonata sopra Sancta Maria* and the motets, *Nigra sum*, *Pulchra es*, *Duo Seraphim*, and *Audi coelum*. It is indicative of the limited state of our knowledge of early seventeenth-century sacred music that even recent biographies of Monteverdi discuss these pieces only in relation to the composer's madrigals and *L'Orfeo*.[71] While similarities between the *sacri concentus* and Monteverdi's secular music cannot be denied, it is important to note that Monteverdi was not the first to employ the monodic style, virtuoso embellishments, quick dotted rhythms, trio textures, echo effects, rhetorical declamation, affective text expression, and orchestral sonatas in sacred music. All of these procedures and styles are found in the motet repertoire in the decade 1600-1610, most noticeably in the last five years of this period. In fact, all five *sacri concentus* are considerably more representative of main currents in early seventeenth-century sacred music than either Monteverdi's psalms or his *Magnificat*s.

Some of the *sacri concentus* are actually based upon individual models by other composers. The *Sonata sopra Sancta Maria*, with its Litany of the Saints intoned eleven times by the *Cantus* part over a large-scale instrumental sonata, is a more elaborate version of a type of piece cultivated in the second half of the *Cinquecento* and the early *Seicento*.[72] Denis Arnold was the first to locate a forerunner in a collection of *Concerti Ecclesiastici* by Arcangelo Crotti of Ferrara published in 1608.[73] Crotti's piece is of much smaller scope than Monteverdi's, and the richness of the latter's imagination in varying rhythmic patterns, textures, sonorities, bass lines, and structural features stands out in comparison with Crotti's pedestrian regularity of phrase lengths, cadences, melodic motives, appearances of the *cantus firmus*, and structural repetitions. Similar differences exist between Monteverdi's *Sonata* and another comparable work by Amante Franzoni of Mantua, published in his *Apparato Musicale* of 1613.[74]

These instrumental sonatas with ostinato *cantus firmus* had their origins in ostinato motets where a vocal ensemble accompanied the repeated motive or chant. Such motets can be traced in French sources as far back as the thirteenth century. Edward Lowinsky has studied ostinato motets from the Renaissance, beginning with Clemens non Papa's *Fremuit spiritu Jesu*, and notes the popularity of this form in Venice.[75] Denis Arnold has called attention to Andrea Gabrieli's *Judica me* of 1587 specifically in connection with the Monteverdi *Sonata*.[76] Arnold's discovery in the surviving part-books of hand-written suggestions for instrumentation in several of the voices establishes a close link between the ostinato motet and the instrumental sonata with litany.[77] Another Venetian motet, *Beatissimus*

Marcus, published by Antonio Gualteri in 1604, employs the same Litany of the Saints as Monteverdi's work, but addresses *"Sancte Marce"* instead of *"Sancta Maria."*[78] The text of the other voices lauds the martyrdom of the patron of Venice, and the piece therefore functions simultaneously as both a song of praise and a supplication.

The instrumental sonata with ostinato motive was also practiced by Giovanni Gabrieli in a composition first described by Christiane Engelbrecht.[79] This piece has a short melody in two voices with the text *"Dulci Jesu patris imago,"* which is repeated intermittently at different tonal levels against a large-scale instrumental sonata of three choirs comprising a total of twenty parts. It is not clear when this piece, found only in manuscript, was written, though its instrumental emphasis suggests that it is probably a late work.

Ostinato motets are also found in the few-voiced motet repertoire after the turn of the century, as witnessed by two examples in a collection of Ignatio Donati published in 1612.[80] One of these pieces pits the Litany of the Saints against the text *"Beatus vir qui inventus est"* sung by a solo vocal quartet, each voice of which is to be positioned in a different part of the church and provided with its own continuo.[81] Donati suits his litany to any saint simply by omitting a specific name and adding the rubric, *"Questo motetto serve per ogni festa di Santo o Santa."* The other motet, which is to be performed in a similar manner, has two ostinato voices continually reiterating the phrase *"Vanitas vanitatum et omnia vanitas."*

At this point some general remarks about the relationship between Monteverdi's *Sonata* and the canzonas and sonatas of Giovanni Gabrieli are in order. Gabrieli is the only other composer of the period to create instrumental works on such an extravagant scale, and it is only natural that many writers have claimed that the *Sonata sopra Sancta Maria* reveals his influence.[82] The multi-sectional structure of Monteverdi's piece, characterized by frequent changes of meter, rhythm, and texture, certainly resembles the organization of many of Gabrieli's canzonas from the posthumous *Canzoni e Sonate* of 1615.[83] But upon comparison of specific compositional details, Monteverdi's independence from the Gabrieli idiom emerges.

One of the most important differences lies in the character of Monteverdi's melodic lines. Throughout the *Sonata* they tend to be conjunct, based on shorter or longer scale patterns. Their rhythms are comparatively even, normally involving only three adjacent rhythmic levels within a single section. The forward impetus of these smoothly flowing melodic lines is further enhanced by the imitative texture.

Gabrieli, by contrast, usually employs shorter, more angular melodic motives with much more rhythmic differentiation. His lines tend to end abruptly, either through cadential harmony or antiphonal exchange with another part. A single melodic phrase may also contain several different types of motives, while Monteverdi maintains much greater motivic consistency, not only within a single phrase, but throughout the entire *Sonata*. This motivic consistency depends upon the repeated use of certain intervals and the universally binding effect of scalar motion. How characteristic of Monteverdi these features are can be seen by comparison with Gabrieli, who rarely employs scalar basses or melodic patterns and whose linear intervals cover a wider range. Canzonas XV and XVIII of Gabrieli's 1615 collection are exceptional in utilizing motives more like those in the Monteverdi work.

Most of Gabrieli's larger canzonas and sonatas are conceived in terms of antiphonal choirs of instruments with frequent, abrupt exchanges of short melodic phrases. Even the smaller canzonas, which rely more heavily on imitative techniques, display their share of antiphonal responses. But Monteverdi uses antiphonal effects rather sparingly; moreover, his interchanges are less clearly articulated than Gabrieli's because of the absence of strong cadential harmony in the bass. Monteverdi's antiphonal passages thus do not beget the sectionalization and discontinuity typical of the Venetian. In addition, Monteverdi's greater interest in melodic and harmonic flow is logically accompanied by more frequent reliance on melodic and harmonic sequences.

Monteverdi's *Sonata*, while scored for eight separate instrumental parts plus basso continuo, has numerous sections in which duets supported by the organ prevail, similar to those in other pieces of the Vespers. Duets of like instruments also occur in many of Gabrieli's canzonas and sonatas, but consistent with his melodic style, they tend to be short and composed of brief motives, and they are often treated antiphonally. These passages are almost invariably ornamental in conception, frequently involving rhythmic values as small as thirty-second notes. Monteverdi's duets, on the other hand, are more extended and form a more integral part of the structure of his work.

Although the *Sonata sopra Sancta Maria* bears a closer relationship to the music of Gabrieli than any other piece in the *Vespro della Beata Vergine*, the foregoing comparisons demonstrate that Monteverdi's style was still very personal, with only the broadest outlines reminiscent of the music of the Venetian organist.

Of the four motets in the 1610 Vespers, *Duo Seraphim* represents by far the most frequently composed text. I have been able to locate some twenty-two published settings besides Monteverdi's in the period 1600-1615.[84] There are doubtless more, and the popularity of these verses goes back at least as far as Victoria's 1583 version.[85] Marc-Antonio Ingegneri, Monteverdi's teacher at Cremona, published a setting in 1589.[86]

Several distinctive ways of treating this text, some originating as early as the Victoria example, were repeated, developed, and expanded in subsequent interpretations well into the seventeenth century. The opening phrase, *"Duo Seraphim clamabant,"* was with rare exceptions set for two voices, even when the overall setting was for many more. Similarly, the beginning of the second half of the text, *"Tres sunt qui testimonium dant,"* was almost invariably cast in three parts. Both traditions were followed by Monteverdi.

The continuation of the second half, *"Pater et Verbum et Spiritus Sanctus,"* was normally subjected to one of two types of treatment. Either the three witnesses, Father, Word, and Holy Spirit, were named successively, each by a single, different voice part, or the entire phrase was organized cumulatively with one voice singing *"Pater,"* two intoning *"Verbum,"* and three following with *"Spiritus Sanctus."* It is the latter method that Monteverdi chose. The succeeding phrase, *"et hi tres unum sunt,"* was interpreted symbolically by many composers with a shift to triple meter, the new signature denoting the proportion 3/1. Monteverdi, however, sought a more dramatic, affective treatment of this line by joining all three voices in unison at *"unum sunt"* and then repeating the entire phrase a step higher. While this is a relatively minor detail, it is typical of Monteverdi to avoid intellectual symbolism in favor of more overt dramatic effects. Giovanni Francesco Anerio's 1609 setting is the only other example to treat these words in a comparable fashion by suddenly reducing the texture from three voices to one.[87]

After the turn of the seventeenth century, when virtuoso ornamentation became a characteristic, at times a *raison d'être*, of some motet collections, the *Duo Seraphim* text with its description of heavenly jubilation often gave rise to a florid style. Although Monteverdi's version is more profusely embellished than any of its counterparts, some of the types of ornamentation he employed do appear in the motet repertoire from 1607 onward. Melismas in these collections often consist of sixteenth notes or dotted rhythms of eighths and sixteenths, with some embellishments comprehending as many as fifty or sixty notes. Occasional groupings of thirty-seconds also appear, as well as the cadential ornament Caccini designates a trill, consisting of the rapid reiteration of a single pitch.[88] Both the trill and melismas in small note values are features of the first motet book of Giovanni Francesco Capello, published in 1610 (see example 9).[89]

Despite the fact that Monteverdi's *Duo Seraphim* has numerous precedents, this composition is illustrative of his propensity for working on a larger, more complex scale than his contemporaries. His *Duo Seraphim* not only is longer than any other setting of this text, but also is more complicated contrapuntally and makes more extensive use of virtuoso ornamental devices than any other few-voiced motet I have yet observed. *Duo Seraphim*, like the psalms, *Magnificats*, and *Sonata*, confirms once more Monteverdi's disposition toward musical opulence and extravagance.

EXAMPLE 9. Giovanni Francesco CAPELLO, *Sancta et immaculata virginitas*

While both the *Sonata sopra Sancta Maria* and *Duo Seraphim* have numerous antecedents, I have been able to locate only one other setting of the text *Audi coelum*, published in 1609 by Ercole Porta.[90] Porta's version of this text is shorter than Monteverdi's by three lines, and since it lacks the phrase "*Omnes hanc ergo sequamur . . .* ," the texture does not burst forth in full choral polyphony at the end like Monteverdi's. But in all of the lines shared by the two pieces, the echo puns are identical (e. g., "*Audi coelum verba mea plena desiderio et perfusa gaudio*" [Echo: "*audio*"]).

Musical relationships between the two compositions are of a more general nature. Porta calls for a pair of sopranos rather than Monteverdi's tenors (the two ranges were often considered interchangeable in the early seventeenth century), but in both works the second voice is reserved exclusively for the echo. While the two settings have numerous structural similarities, a comparison of parallel passages reveals Monteverdi's much more concentrated sense of melodic direction (see examples 10a and 10b). Where Porta meanders aimlessly, Monteverdi avails himself of the

EXAMPLE 10a. Ercole PORTA, *Audi coelum*

EXAMPLE 10b. MONTEVERDI, *Audi coelum*

recitative style and rising sequences to shape an intense, goal-directed phrase. Indicative of the sophistication and complexity of Monteverdi's musical thought is that the brief passage in example 10b also functions on a larger architectural level. This phrase is only the first in a series of three, each of which is a variation upon the preceding one. Porta, on the other hand, continues on to a new, unrelated melodic idea. It is a distinguishing characteristic of Monteverdi throughout the Vespers, indeed, throughout his *oeuvre*, that he carefully integrates details of melody and harmony with broader structural considerations.

Monteverdi's *Audi coelum* also differs from Porta's in its extensive ornamentation, especially in some of the echoes. Porta's rendering, by contrast, is mostly syllabic and shows little of Monteverdi's interest in appropriate text declamation and affective expression.

Although the texts of the two remaining motets, *Nigra sum* and *Pulchra es*, were reasonably popular in the late sixteenth and early seventeenth centuries, few significant traditions in the musical setting of particular words and phrases seem to have evolved.[91] In the case of pieces with the incipit *Nigra sum*, there are so many textual variants, many bearing little resemblance to Monteverdi's version or to one another, that it was impossible for traditions of word treatment to develop. The text *Pulchra es*, derived like *Nigra sum* from the Song of Songs, does not seem to have inspired musical composition as frequently. It enjoyed some popularity in Rome, as witnessed by a 1588 setting of Palestrina and early seventeenth-century interpretations by Agazzari and G. F. Anerio. It was also set to music by northerners such as Banchieri, Usper, Monteverdi, and others. A device encountered in many of these compositions, including Monteverdi's, is special harmonic emphasis on the word *suavis* in the opening line *"Pulchra es amica mea suavis et decora."* The rendering of this word usually involved some kind of chromatic alteration relative to the first part of the phrase. A few other common approaches to specific textual passages are also evident, but none is of sufficient importance to detain us here.

Monteverdi's *Nigra sum* and *Audi coelum* are especially notable for their utilization of the recitative style. Monteverdi was by no means the first to apply the recitative to sacred music, however. Two composers mentioned above who were strongly influenced by Caccini, Ottavio Durante and Don Severo Bonini, both employed recitative in earlier sacred publications.[92] The opening of Durante's *Filiae Jerusalem* may be quoted as an illustration (see example 11). Like Monteverdi, Durante did not adhere exclusively to the one style but mixed it with arioso. Bonini followed much the same practice.

Two other motet books that appeared in the same year as Monteverdi's Vespers deserve at least passing mention. These are the first sacred publications of Alessandro Grandi and Giovanni Francesco Capello, both

EXAMPLE 11. Ottavio DURANTE, *Filiae Jerusalem*

of which contain pieces that either closely resemble some of Monteverdi's motets or share a number of distinctive features with them.[93] Both collections emphasize again the intimate relationship between Monteverdi's *sacri concentus* and developments discernible elsewhere in the motet repertoire of the early seventeenth century.

V

The remaining two pieces of the *Vespro*, the respond *Domine ad adiuvandum* and the hymn *Ave maris stella*, further confirm Monteverdi's penchant for grandiloquent forms of expression. Many Vesper collections begin with the Vesper respond, but it is invariably a short, modest piece in keeping with the brevity of its text. *Falsobordone* and measured chordal homophony are frequently used techniques. Monteverdi himself draws on the tradition of *falsobordone*, but when this is superimposed on an adaptation of the toccata from *L'Orfeo*, and the entire structure is enlarged by the addition of triple meter *ritornelli*, a much more extended and elaborate composition ensues with a wholly new aesthetic purpose. The respond becomes a large-scale vocal and instrumental *sinfonia*, introducing the magnificence of the entire Vesper service with its own musical brilliance. As with other pieces of the *Vespro*, Monteverdi has discerned the possibility of combining originally simple types of music with divergent purposes to fulfill both the required liturgical function and the need for an appropriately ostentatious introduction to his sumptuous collection.

Hymn settings, in contrast to the respond, are extremely rare in publications of Vesper music, and Monteverdi's inclusion of *Ave maris stella* is an indication of his wish to supply a complete musical service.[94] His setting is based on a strophic format, frequently encountered in hymn collections of the sixteenth century, consisting of harmonization of the *cantus firmus*, which remains in the topmost voice throughout. But as we have seen so often, Monteverdi is never content with a simple and unassuming structure, and he elaborates on this basic plan in an ingenious fashion. The details of his setting have been described in chapter III and need not be repeated here; I need only observe that an unpretentious, traditional technique has once again been combined with modern elements to produce a piece of larger than normal dimensions and complexity.

VI

A summary overview of the comparisons made in the preceding sections of this essay reaffirms that different aspects of Monteverdi's *Vespro* have different relationships with the contemporary repertoire. The contents of the 1610 print place it within a small group of collections devoted to music for a single category of Vesper feasts. These collections are not applicable to as many feasts as the mainstream of Vesper publications, but most of them attempt to provide a greater quantity of polyphonic music for the feasts they serve. Within this specialized repertoire, Monteverdi's is the only collection before Agostini's Marian Vespers of 1619 (which itself may well have been influenced by Monteverdi) to intersperse motets between psalms and to include a setting of an appropriate hymn.

Monteverdi's approach to musical style is considerably more inventive and individualistic than his selection of pieces for the collection. The psalms and *Magnificat*s draw not only from traditional, even outmoded, procedures in their respective genres, but also from the most progressive tendencies, especially those originating in publications of few-voiced motets. Monteverdi's complex synthesis of highly diverse materials and techniques results in more expansive and variegated compositions than appear anywhere else in the contemporary Vesper repertoire. The *Magnificat*s in particular exhibit a unique combination of elements. In sheer musical magnificence, the only works comparable to Monteverdi's psalms, *Magnificat*s, respond, and hymn are the late motets of Giovanni Gabrieli. Gabrieli, however, shows little interest in Vesper music and the details of his style differ substantially from Monteverdi's.

The five *sacri concentus*, on the other hand, are commensurate with developments in the motet and instrumental canzona and sonata after the turn of the seventeenth century. But even in his motets and the *Sonata sopra Sancta Maria*, Monteverdi's large dimensions, virtuoso embellishments, structural cohesion, and rhetorical treatment of texts far surpass the achievements of most other composers.

VII

The very originality of the *Vespro della Beata Vergine* should greatly facilitate a study of the impact and influence of Monteverdi's publication on subsequent Vesper compositions. It is probable that any Vesper collection from the years immediately after 1610 that exhibits characteristics of Monteverdi's music not found in the repertoire prior to that year has been directly or indirectly influenced by him. The discussion of this material will be limited here to the decade 1610-1620.

Two collections published in 1611, one by Don Giovanni Flaccomio[95] and the other by Don Grisostomo Rubiconi,[96] already reveal probable Monteverdian influence. Although only five of nine part-books survive from each collection, they contain enough rubrics and other indications of style and structure to determine with reasonable accuracy the character of the music. In both publications psalm and Magnificat settings for double choir are subdivided into sections of contrasting sonority, sometimes entailing a soloist or ensemble of two, three, or four voices. Table I illustrates the organization of Rubiconi's *Dixit Dominus* as itemized in the original print.

TABLE I

Dixit Dominus	basso e 2 tenori
Donec ponam inimicos	alto e doi soprani
Virgam virtutis	alto, basso e tenor
Tecum principium	alto e basso
Iuravit Dominus	a 2 canti e a 8
Dominus a dextris tuis	basso e doi tenori
Iudicabit in nationibus	a doi bassi
De torrente	doi bassi e 2 canti
Gloria Patri	a 8
Sicut erat	[a 8]

Rubiconi's reliance on few-voiced textures is even more palpable than Monteverdi's. The full eight-voice choir appears in only a single interior section and the Doxology. In the other verses, the voices are not always matched in pairs of the same range as with Monteverdi. Rubiconi employs a greater variety of combinations, though at times he pits two soloists in one register against a third in another (cf. Monteverdi's *Dixit Dominus*).

Flaccomio is equally attracted to contrasts in sonority and texture. His *Nisi Dominus*, for example, marked "*da concierto*," alternates between odd-numbered verses distributed among soloists from the first choir (descending from soprano through tenor) and even-numbered verses set *à 4* for the second choir. The two verses of the Doxology are each assigned to one of the four-voice ensembles. The influence of the *alternatim* technique, at the basis of Monteverdi's *Dixit Dominus*, is also evident here. In his *Magnificat*, Flaccomio adds instrumental coloring, requesting doubling "*cum corneta*" and "*cum basonicco*" in two separate duos.

These extended, sectionalized compositions, with their conspicuous changes in texture and their dependence on solo voices, are apparently direct responses to Monteverdi's example, since there are no other precedents in the Vesper repertoire. Not all peculiarities of the *Vespro*, however, were equally influential, for neither Rubiconi's nor Flaccomio's surviving part-books give any hint of the psalm tone, nor does their solo writing approach Monteverdi's extraordinary virtuosity. As we shall see, the psalm tone was avoided as assiduously after 1610 as it had been before; indeed, Monteverdi himself never used it as a systematic *cantus firmus* again.[97] The absence of virtuosity in Rubiconi's and Flaccomio's collections may be attributed to the fact that few places in Italy had the quality of singers available in Mantua and Ferrara. Even in Venice Gabrieli provided comparatively modest parts for his soloists.

A rare instance of the plainchant in a significant role is found in a collection of music for Holy Week by Giovanni Francesco Capello, published in 1612.[98] Capello's eight-voice setting of the Canticle of Zacharia, *Benedictus Dominus Deus Israel*, accompanied solely by the basso continuo, carries the rubric "*Del primo Tono in Sol sopra il Canto fermo.*" No other composition I have seen aside from Monteverdi's psalms and *Magnificat*s uses a cantus firmus so extensively as to call attention to the fact in print. The plainchant melody for the canticle closely resembles a psalm tone and is repeated for each verse of the text in the same manner as the psalm chants. A large portion of Capello's piece consists of chordal harmonization of the *cantus firmus*, which appears successively in different voices and alternately at its initial tonal level and a fourth below.

Many aspects of Capello's music bear a remarkably close relationship to Monteverdi.[99] His motets have already been mentioned, and in his 1612 *Lamentationi*, *obbligato* instruments are prominently featured. Another composition from this collection, the psalm *Miserere mei Deus*, is scarcely conceivable without the example of Monteverdi's *Vespro*. This five-voice setting depends heavily on solo writing and an instrumental ensemble comprising a *violetta*, two violas, a *violone*, and *chitaroni*. The sectionalization of Capello's psalm is as pronounced as any of Monteverdi's. *Ritornelli* are interspersed throughout the piece and the instrumental ensemble also serves in whole or in part as an accompaniment in several sections. Two imitative duets closely resemble Monteverdi's duet style (see example 12). The segments for solo voices approximate the recitative passages of *Nigra sum* and *Audi coelum* (see example 13). Virtuoso embellishments are lacking, but they are abundant in other pieces in the *Lamentationi*, as well as in Capello's 1610 collection of motets.[100]

Among the most striking illustrations of Monteverdi's influence are the *Salmi Intieri* of 1613 and the *Messa, Salmi, et Motetti Concertati* of 1615 by Don Antonio Burlini, from sometime in 1612 organist at Monteoliveto Maggiore in Siena.[101] The *Salmi Intieri* are large-scale, through-composed, and highly diverse settings of considerable musical interest. Burlini's four-voice choir is supported not only by an organ continuo but also at times by separate parts for an *instrumento acuto* and an *instrumento grave*, both "*se*

EXAMPLE 12. Giovanni Francesco CAPELLO, *Miserere*

EXAMPLE 13. Giovanni Francesco CAPELLO, *Miserere*

piace.'' Each verse of a psalm is confined to a distinct section and these sections are differentiated from one another by significant changes of style. Solo and duet textures are frequently encountered, though in these segments all parts may briefly combine for a four-voice passage. Imitative duets with instrumental accompaniment are also common. *Falsibordoni* and block chordal style appear occasionally, and some passages shift from the prevailing duple meter to triple time. Within a single section the verse is often split into segments of only a few words, repeated several times before the text continues.

Not only is the general character of Burlini's *Salmi Intieri* reminiscent of the *Vespro della Beata Vergine*, but there are a few passages that appear to be directly imitative of Monteverdi. The opening of Burlini's *Laudate pueri* employs the same psalm tone as Monteverdi's *Dixit Dominus*, with its characteristic dip to the seventh degree both at the beginning and part way through the chant. As in *Dixit Dominus*, Burlini's plainsong serves as a subject for imitation, leading to a full-voiced chordal passage (see example 14). But Monteverdi's six voices, two of them carrying a countersubject, result in a more complicated texture than Burlini's four. In the *Quia fecit* of Burlini's first canticle, the Magnificat tone emerges in long note values in a solo voice accompanied by the organ and a pair of instruments, a procedure directly comparable to the *Quia respexit* of Monteverdi's *Magnificat à 7* (see example 15). Similarly, the *Gloria Patri* of Burlini's setting is a florid echo piece analogous to Monteverdi's.

EXAMPLE 14. Antonio BURLINI, *Laudate pueri*

EXAMPLE 15. Antonio BURLINI, *Magnificat*

The second canticle of the *Salmi Intieri* is similar in style to the first, although there is more emphasis on the full chorus. The *Et exultavit* of this piece bears a remarkable resemblance to the *Et exultavit* of Monteverdi's seven-voice *Magnificat*. Both versions begin with a melismatic passage in two-voice imitation followed by sequential repetition at a higher level (Monteverdi's sequence rises by a fifth, Burlini's by a fourth). In both settings there is a subsequent slowing of the pace at *"spiritus meus"* succeeded by a short melismatic figure treated imitatively at *"in deo."* Although Burlini dispenses with the Magnificat tone and calls for four voices rather than Monteverdi's two, the derivation of his setting of this verse is obvious (see example 16, pp. 165-166).

Despite the parallels between Burlini's and Monteverdi's *Magnificat*s, significant differences are also apparent. Burlini employs his full vocal ensemble (only four voices in comparison to Monteverdi's seven) much more often, especially as the piece progresses. Burlini's instruments function differently too; their style is less ornamental and, like the voices, they do not approach Monteverdi's characteristic virtuosity. The instruments also perform a *sinfonia* before the beginning of the first *Magnificat*, following the example of several motets in Giovanni Gabrieli's *Sacrae Symphoniae* of 1615. The Gabrieli collection, of course, postdates Burlini's, but as noted earlier, Gabrieli died in 1612 and many of his works were probably widely known before publication. Burlini himself was resident in Venice prior to his removal to Siena in 1612.[102]

Burlini's collection of 1615 is somewhat more conservative, while still revealing Monteverdi's influence. The psalms and *Magnificat* are for eight-voice *cori spezzati*, and homophonic textures and antiphonal effects are correspondingly prominent. Nevertheless, there are intervening passages for one, two, three, and four voices in the first choir, all in a modest vocal style. In addition to the organ continuo, a part for a single *obbligato* instrument is provided. These pieces, like those of the *Salmi Intieri*, are large-scale works of considerable stylistic variety whose overall dimensions reflect the impact of the *Vespro della Beata Vergine.*

Among Magnificats published in motet books, one by Don Serafino Patta from 1613 displays Monteverdi's influence in its highly varied and complex structure as well as in some individual details.[103] This five-voice piece shows a heavy concentration on solos and duets in the virtuoso style, with only a minority of the verses requiring the full ensemble (see example 17). Some of the few-voiced sections are cast in *falsibordoni*, but others are reminiscent of the solo writing of Ottavio Durante. The duets tend to be imitative and comparable to Monteverdi's (see example 18, p. 168). The Magnificat tone even appears in long note values at the beginning of the *Deposuit*, while the *Gloria Patri* employs a choral echo.

EXAMPLE 16. Antonio BURLINI, *Magnificat* (cont. on next page)

EXAMPLE 16 continued.

EXAMPLE 17. Serafino PATTA, *Magnificat*

In 1613 Monteverdi assumed his new post as *maestro di cappella* at St. Mark's in Venice, and various aspects of his music seem to have had their effect on a few composers in the Venetian state shortly thereafter. The 1614 psalms of Francesco Usper, organist at the Church of San Salvatore in Venice, manifest an unusual interest in thin textures.[104] Usper's *Laudate pueri* in particular, marked *concertato senza intonatione*, utilizes its full five voices only at the conclusion of a few sections. Imitative duets prevail instead, and passagework is frequent.

Much grander in design is a 1616 collection by Amadio Freddi of Treviso.[105] An *obbligato cornetto* and *violino* accompany the vocal parts in some pieces and perform additional *sinfonie* in others. The psalm and Magnificat settings imitate Monteverdi in their elaborate style and in their variety of textures, rhythms, meters, and melodic patterns. Change and contrast are almost continuous in these pieces. Short passages of text, sometimes only a few words, are isolated for individual musical treatment. Soloists are juxtaposed with the five-voice *tutti* and chordal writing is interchanged with imitation. Even the psalm tone appears with some frequency, though without the pervasive structural function of Monteverdi. The passages for soloists, however, shun vocal virtuosity.

It is in the collections of Usper and Freddi that the influence of Monteverdi began to supersede that of Giovanni Gabrieli in Venetian music. The antiphonal style shows evidence of yielding to the thinner textures and soloistic passages of San Marco's new *maestro di cappella*, although neither Usper nor Freddi made the extraordinary virtuoso demands that Monteverdi did.

Gabrieli normally confined antiphonal contrasts to his multi-choir pieces, while in his works for fewer voices the textures fluctuate in accord with sixteenth-century practice—through the entrance and exit of parts without cadences and without breaking the continuity of the forward motion. The

EXAMPLE 18. Serafino PATTA, *Magnificat*

five-voice pieces of Usper and Freddi, however, are much more clearly sectionalized by means of sudden contrasts and deliberate discontinuities. In this respect they follow Monteverdi and arrive at the *concertato* style without indulging in the massed antiphony of Gabrieli. Gabrieli's gigantic polychoral works were rapidly eclipsed with the advent of Monteverdi in Venice, and variety, contrast, and color became dependent upon factors other than large masses of sound. As a result, Usper and especially Freddi reveal their progressive tendencies not through antiphony, but by their emphasis on thin textures, solo voices and instruments, vocal and instrumental duets, and sudden juxtapositions of contrasting rhythms, textures, and sonorities.

All of the collections heretofore discussed emanated from northern Italy, where Vesper psalms had enjoyed a special prominence throughout the sixteenth century. The papal seat of Rome, on the other hand, had shown little interest in polyphonic psalmody, either before or after the Council of Trent. There are relatively few Vesper psalms in Roman manuscripts and prints of the *Cinquecento*, and it is only in the early seventeenth century that collections of Vesper music began to proliferate there. It is hardly surprising, therefore, that the modern approach to Vespers as established by Monteverdi and his followers did not appear in the post-Tridentine environment of Rome until 1620. In that year an unusual collection, containing both conservative and modern settings of psalms and Magnificats, was published by Paolo Tardito.[106] The modern compositions are double-choir pieces with the addition of a lute to the first chorus and a *cornetto* to the second. In these works Tardito's style does not differ significantly from Amadio Freddi's. Despite the division into two four-voice choirs, antiphonal effects are subordinate to such techniques as abrupt contrasts and thin textures. Solo duet passages, especially duets for voices in the same range, suggest the influence of Monteverdi. Virtuoso writing is much more in evidence than in Freddi's compositions, but it does not quite approach Monteverdian proportions (see example 19).

There is little to be gained by attempting to weigh the relative impact of Monteverdi's psalms and *Magnificats*, for it is apparent from the collections of Burlini, Freddi, and Tardito that these composers did not distinguish stylistically between the two liturgical genres as Monteverdi did. The greater consistency of style among their psalms and *Magnificats* indicates that the latter were probably influenced as much by Monteverdi's psalms as by his canticles. All three composers utilized the full ensemble much more often in their *Magnificats* than did Monteverdi, and their solo writing was more restrained, avoiding his extravagant ornamentation. Although all three employed *obbligato* instruments, the instruments discharge a more modest function, adding their color to the total sonority, but assuming very little individuality or idiomatic purpose. The *Magnificats* of Burlini, Freddi, and Tardito imitate Monteverdi's in their grand and

EXAMPLE 19. Paolo TARDITO, *Magnificat*

ostentatious manner based on clearly articulated contrasts, but they do not follow him in his concentration on intimate sonorities and relegation of the chorus to a merely framing role.

Despite the authority exerted by Monteverdi's unique Vesper music in the decade after 1610, it must be stressed that the publications revealing this influence are an exceptional few in a vast repertoire which continued and developed oblivious to the example of Italy's foremost composer. This conclusion is not unexpected, given the widespread devotion to Vesper music and the practical use of Vesper collections in surroundings much more humble than the court of the Gonzagas or the church of Venice's patron saint. The fact is that few churches commanded the vocal and instrumental resources required for such opulent music. But as the taste for elaborate *concertato* settings grew over the years, so did the abilities of many performers and churches to cope with the new styles. The lengthy, varied compositions of Monteverdi, Rubiconi, Flaccomio, Burlini, Patta, Freddi, and Tardito gradually inspired greater quantities of comparable pieces, and by the mid-1630s extensive Vesper psalms and Magnificats employing instruments and soloists permeated the repertoire. After the middle of the century Bologna in particular became a center for this kind of music under Mauritio Cazzati, the prolific *maestro di cappella* of San Petronio.[107]

But while the *concertato* style unquestionably informed a large part of the Vesper repertoire of the seventeenth century, it is also true that it did not drive out altogether the older, more conservative styles, which continued unabated alongside the modern. Numerous collections of psalms for five voices or for double choir *"per tutte le solennità"* testify to the continuation of traditions and techniques formulated in the sixteenth century and still practiced widely. The stylistic dichotomy between the old and the new witnessed at the beginning of the *Seicento* by so many theorists and composers, including Monteverdi himself, was still in evidence as the century progressed.

Nevertheless, the importance of Monteverdi's Vespers in the development of the large-scale *concertato* has been securely established. The influence of his music, which at first proceeded slowly, gradually accumulated momentum as more and more composers in the 1620s and 1630s were attracted to the elaborate style. And Monteverdi, of course, made further contributions to the tide with later Vesper psalms of his own. But as time went on, his influence undoubtedly became less direct, with many composers responding to the stimulus of his followers rather than to Monteverdi himself. This may already have been the case with regard to Tardito in 1620. What had begun as a highly individual approach to music for Vespers on feasts of the Virgin gradually became a general aesthetic outlook shared by many composers, most likely without any precise knowledge of its origins. As the elaborate *concertato* style of Vesper music spread, it also influenced mass composition and inevitably commingled with other modern developments. It was out of these streams that evolved the trends which were to dominate sacred music for two centuries to come.

NOTES

This essay was originally published in *Analecta Musicologica* **15** (1975): 29-86. It has been revised and updated for republication in this volume with the kind permission of the editor of *Analecta*, Dr. Friedrich Lippmann.

1. The only attempt at a comprehensive survey of Italian sacred music of this period is by Jerome Roche, "North Italian Liturgical Music in the early 17th century; its Evolution around 1600 and its Development until the Death of Monteverdi" (Ph.D. dissertation, Cambridge University, 1967), which is currently being revised by the author for publication. Among the most important articles devoted to the *Vespro* in recent years are Hans F. Redlich, "Claudio Monteverdi: Some Problems of Textual Interpretation," *Musical Quarterly* **41**, no. 1 (January 1955): 66-75; Denis Stevens, "Where are the Vespers of Yesteryear?" *Musical Quarterly* **47**, no. 3 (July 1961): 315-330; Giuseppe Biella, "La 'Messa,' il 'Vespro' e i 'Sacri Concenti' di Claudio Monteverdis nella stampa Amadino dell'anno 1610," *Musica Sacra*, serie seconda **9** (1964): 104-115; Denis Arnold, "Notes on two Movements of the Monteverdi 'Vespers,'" *Monthly Musical Record* **84** (March/April 1954): 59-66; Arnold, "Monteverdi's Church Music: some Venetian Traits," *Monthly Musical Record* **88** (May/June 1958): 83-91; Arnold, "The Monteverdi 'Vespers'—a Postscript," *Musical Times* **104** (January 1963): 24-25; Arnold, "Monteverdi and the Technique of 'Concertato,'" *The Amor Artis Bulletin* **6**, no. 3 (April 1967): 1-8; Stephen Bonta, "Liturgical Problems in Monteverdi's Marian Vespers," *Journal of the American Musicological Society* **20**, no. 1 (Spring 1967): 87-106; Wolfgang Osthoff, "Unità liturgica e artistica nei *Vespri* del 1610," *Rivista italiana di Musicologia* **2**, no. 2 (1967): 314-327; Jürgen Jürgens, "Urtext und Affführungspraxis bei Monteverdis *Orfeo* und *Marien-Vesper*," *Claudio Monteverdi e il suo Tempo, Atti del Congresso internazionale di Studi monteverdiani, May 3-May 7, 1968*, ed. Raffaello Monterosso (Verona: La Stamperia Valdonega, 1969), pp. 269-304; Andreas Holschneider, "Zur Aufführungspraxis der Marien-Vesper von Monteverdi," *Hamburger Jahrbuch für Musikwissenschaft*, vol. I (Hamburg: Karl Dieter Wagner, 1974), pp. 59-68; and Iain Fenlon, "The Monteverdi Vespers," *Early Music* **5**, no. 3 (July 1977): 380-387. See also the liner notes to the Telefunken recording of the *Vespro della Beata Vergine* written by Wolfgang Osthoff, the liner notes to the Musical Heritage Society's recording of the *Vespro* by Denis Stevens, and the preface to Denis Stevens, ed., *Claudio Monteverdi: Vespers* (London: Novello and Company Ltd., 1961). The best modern edition of the Vespers, though lacking the six-voice *Magnificat* and needing correction of some details, is by Gottfried Wolters, *Claudio Monteverdi: Vesperae Beatae Mariae Virginis* (Wolfenbüttel and Zürich: Möseler Verlag, 1966). I have not yet seen a new version, edited by Jürgen Jürgens (Vienna: Universal Edition, 1977). For a review by Denis Arnold of this edition, see *Early Music* **6**, no. 3 (July 1978): 459-464.

2. See Adam Adrio, *Die Anfänge des geistlichen Konzerts* (Berlin: Junker und Dünnhaupt, 1935); Hugo Leichtentritt, *Geschichte der Motette*, vol. II of "Kleine Hand-

bücher der Musikgeschichte" (Leipzig: Breitkopf und Härtel, 1908); Hans F. Redlich, "Early Baroque Church Music," *The Age of Humanism, 1540-1630,* ed. by Gerald Abraham, vol. IV of "The New Oxford History of Music" (London: Oxford University Press, 1968), pp. 520-546; Jerome Roche, "The Duet in early seventeenth-century Italian Church Music," *Proceedings of the Royal Musical Association* (1967), pp. 33-50; William H. Schempf, "Polychoral Magnificats from H. Praetorius to H. Schütz (Ph.D. dissertation, University of Rochester, 1960); and James Foster Armstrong, "The Vesper Psalms and Magnificats of Maurizio Cazzati" (Ph.D. dissertation, Harvard University, 1969). I have also written a paper entitled "The Development and Diffusion of Italian Sacred Monody, 1600-1620: A Preliminary Study," to be published in *Rassegna di studi musicali.*

3. This question is discussed in most of the articles listed in note 1. See also the Introduction, pp. 2-4, and James Armstrong, "The *Antiphonae, seu Sacrae Cantiones* (1613) of Giovanni Francesco Anerio: A Liturgical Study," *Analecta Musicologica* 14 (1974): 89-150.

4. *Di Adriano et di Jachet i Salmi appertinenti alli Vesperi Per tutte le Feste Dell'anno, Parte a versi, & parte spezzadi Accomodati da Cantare a uno & a duoi Chori . . . In Venetia Apresso di Antonio Gardane. 1550.* See RISM, 1550[1].

5. As an example one may cite the *Salmi Interi à Cinque Voci* of Orfeo Vecchi, published in Milan in 1598. The print contains sixteen psalms, two *Magnificats,* the four Marian antiphons, and two sets of *falsibordoni.* See Claudio Sartori, *Bibliografia della Musica Strumentale Italiana Stampata in Italia fino al 1700,* 2 vols. (Florence: Leo S. Olschki, 1952-1968), vol. I, p. 101.

6. A case in point is Giovanni Matteo Asola's *Vespertina omnium solemnitatum psalmodia* of 1590. This very large collection consists of fifteen Vesper psalms, two *Magnificats,* one Marian antiphon, a complete Mass Ordinary, and five motets. See Claudio Sartori, *Assisi, La cappella della basilica di S. Francesco. Catalogo del Fondo Musicale nella Biblioteca Comunale di Assisi,* vol. I of "Bibliotheca musicae" (Milan: Istituto Editoriale Italiano, 1962), p. 28.

7. *Messa, Salmi, Motetti, et Magnificat, a Tre Chori. Di Antonio Mortaro da Brescia . . . In Milano appresso l'herede di Simon Tini, & Gio. Francesco Besozzi. 1599.* See Emilio Maggini, *Lucca, Biblioteca del Seminario. Catalogo delle musiche stampate e manoscritto del fondo antico,* vol. III of "Bibliotheca musicae" (Milan: Istituto Editoriale Italiano, 1965), p. 162.

8. Stephen Bonta has coined the term "Regular" to refer to those liturgical items that fall between the Ordinary and the Proper, such as groups of Vesper psalms that remain the same for all feasts of a certain category, but do not serve all feasts throughout the year. See Bonta, "Liturgical Problems," p. 90.

9. *Musices Liber Primus Hymnos, Magnificat, Salves, Motecta, Psalmos, aliquae diversa cantica complectens. Venetiis, apud A. Gardanum, 1565.* See Argia Bertini, *Roma, Biblioteca Corsiniana e dell'Accademia nazionale dei Lincei: catalogo dei fondi musicali Chiti e Corsiniano,* vol. II of "Bibliotheca musicae" (Milan: Istituto Editoriale Italiano, 1964), p. 36.

10. *Missa, Psalmi ad Vesperas Dominicales, Magnificat et Psalmorum modulationes,*

quae passim in Ecclesiis usurpantur. Auctore Orpheo Vecchio Medio. Presb. apud S. Mariae a Scala Capellae Magistro. Octonis vocibus. Mediolani, apud Franciscum et haeredes Simonis Tini. 1590. See Maggini, *Lucca, Biblioteca del Seminario,* p. 197.

11. For a complete list of these collections along with their contents, see Jeffrey Kurtzman, "The Monteverdi Vespers of 1610 and their Relationship with Italian Sacred Music of the Early Seventeenth Century" (Ph.D. dissertation, University of Illinois at Urbana-Champaign, 1972), Appendices B and C, pp. 414-425.

12. See the list of contents in the Introduction, p. 2.

13. *Messa Salmi per i Vesperi, et Motetti, a otto voci Con il Basso per sonar nel'Organo, di Francesco Terriera da Conegliano. Libro Primo . . . In Venetia, Appresso Giacomo Vincenti. 1601.* See Sergio Paganelli, "Catalogo delle opere musicali a stampa dal'500 al'700 conservate presso la Biblioteca Comunale di Cesena," *Collectanea historiae musicae* 2 (1957): 337.

14. *Ioannis Righi Civitatis Mirandulae Canonici, ac Musices prefecti: Missa, Motecta, Psalmi ad vesperas, cum duobus Canticis, ac Litanijs in omnibus B. Mariae Virginis Festivitatibus, Octo Vocibus decantanda . . . Venetiis, Apud Iacobum Vincentium, 1606.* See Francesco Bussi, *Piacenza, Archivio del Duomo. Catalogo del Fondo Musicale,* vol. V of "Bibliotheca musicae" (Milan: Istituto Editoriale Italiano, 1967), pp. 89-90.

15. *Il Secondo Libro de Concerti Ecclesiastici à otto voci di Pompeo Signorucci I. C. Accademico Unisono di Perugia, Maestro di Capella nel Duomo di Pisa. Cioè Salmi, Magnificat, Motetti, & una Messa dell'Ottavo Tono . . . Et con il Basso continuato, potendosi cantare in Capella, e sonar nell'Organo con ogni sorte d'Instrumento. Opera Undecima. In Venetia, Appresso Giacomo Vincenti. 1608.* See Emil Bohn, *Bibliographie der Musik-Druckwerke bis 1700 welche in der Stadtbibliothek, der Bibliothek des Acad. Inst. für Kirchenmusik, und der K. und Universitäts-Bibliothek zu Breslau aufbewahrt werden* (Berlin: A. Cohn, 1883), p. 397.

16. See the Introduction, pp. 2-4. Of the authors of the articles cited in notes 1 and 3, Redlich, Biella, and Stevens present the negative arguments, while Bonta, Osthoff, Armstrong, and to a lesser extent Arnold provide evidence favoring the antiphon-substitute theory. Bonta's "Liturgical Problems" and Armstrong's "The *Antiphonae*" are by far the most comprehensive treatments of the subject.

17. Bonta brings to bear contemporary theoretical treatises, while Armstrong's study of Anerio's *Antiphonae* provides evidence of the practice of substituting polyphonic motets without strictly liturgical texts in place of officially sanctioned antiphons. Robert J. Snow has suggested in personal conversation, however, that Anerio's *Antiphonae are* the officially sanctioned texts for certain mendicant orders. Much work remains to be done on the vagaries of pre-Tridentine and post-Tridentine liturgy.

18. *Salmi della Madonna Magnificat à 3. voci. Hinno Ave Maris Stella, Antifone à una, 2. & 3. voci. Et Motetti Tutti Concertati. Di Paolo Agostino Maestro di Cappella in San Lorenzo in Damaso, Discepolo, & Genero di Gio. Bernardino Nanini. Con il Basso continuo per sonare . . . Libro Primo. In Roma, Per Luca Antonio Soldi. 1619.* See Gaetano Gaspari, *Catalogo della Biblioteca Musicale G. B. Martini di Bologna,* reprint ed. by Napoleone Fanti, Oscar Mischiati, and Luigi Tagliavini, 5 vols. (Bologna: Arnaldo Forni, 1961), vol. II, p. 156 (hereafter cited as Gaspari).

19. Bonta, "Liturgical Problems," pp. 95-96.

20. Specifically, in Verona, Biblioteca Capitolare, Ms. 759. While no systematic study of manuscript Vesper psalms has yet been made, it is clear that numerous sixteenth-century manuscripts group these four psalms in the same order. In some manuscripts the distribution of tones is different from that described above, but many manuscripts do not list the tones at all and may agree with the order given here. Codex III of the Archivio Capitolare of Modena presents this particular series of psalms twice, each time with one discrepancy in the ascending numerical tonal sequence. See David Crawford, "Vespers Polyphony at Modena's Cathedral in the First Half of the Sixteenth Century" (Ph.D. dissertation, University of Illinois, 1967), pp. 75-78.

21. Robert J. Snow's research in this field indicates much more diversity in liturgical practice than is reflected by the *Liber Usualis*.

22. *L'Organo Suonarino di Adriano Banchieri Bolognese . . . In Venetia appresso Ricciardo Amadino. 1605.* Facsimile edition published by Frits Knuf, Amsterdam (n.d.).

23. Ibid., p. 52.

24. Ibid., p. 54 (*Confitebor tibi*) and p. 56 (*Dixit Dominus*).

25. Bonta, "Liturgical Problems," pp. 95-96. Bonta has recently studied the use of instrumental music in the liturgical service, including its role as a substitute for both Ordinary and Proper items. See Bonta, "The Uses of the Sonata da Chiesa," *Journal of the American Musicological Society* 22, no. 1 (Spring 1969): 54-84. See also Armstrong, "*The Antiphonae.*" A small number of contemporary letters, descriptions of performances, and official documents similarly attest to the role of motets in the Vesper service. See the passages quoted in Bonta, "Liturgical Problems," pp. 97-98; Osthoff, "Unità liturgica," p. 319; and Arnold, "The Monteverdi Vespers," p. 25.

26. See the discussion of this issue in the Introduction, pp. 2-4, and chapter I, pp. 28-40.

27. A discussion of the use of instruments in both motets and Vesper music follows below.

28. See chapter I for a fuller discussion of the old and new styles in the print as well as an assessment of possible performances in Mantua.
I wish to acknowledge the assistance of Prof. William Harris of Middlebury College for his comments on the grammatical structure of Monteverdi's title and the distinction between "*ad Sacella*" and "*ad Ecclesiam.*"

29. Translated in Oliver Strunk, *Source Readings in Music History* (New York: W. W. Norton & Company, Inc., 1950), pp. 269-270. James Armstrong, in an as yet unpublished article entitled "How to Compose a Psalm: Ponzio and Cerone Compared," demonstrates Cerone's dependence on Pietro Ponzio's *Ragionamento di musica* of 1588. I am grateful to Prof. Armstrong for the opportunity to study this article prior to its publication.

30. See the extensive discussion of the Council and the mass in chapter II of Lewis Lockwood, *The Counter-Reformation and the Masses of Vincenzo Ruffo*, vol. II of "Studi di Musica Veneta" (Venice: Fondazione Giorgio Cini, 1970), pp. 74-135. The

Council's canon for the mass is quoted in Gustave Reese, *Music in the Renaissance* (New York: W. W. Norton and Company, Inc., 1954), p. 449.

31. In *Del Reverendo M. D. Gio. Giacomo Gastoldi, Maestro di Capella nella Chiesa Ducale di Santa Barbara di Mantoa. Tutti li Salmi che nelle Solennità dell'anno al Vespro si cantano, à otto voci. Con duoi Cantici della B. Vergine, uno del Settimo tuono, & uno del Secondo tuono, che risponde in Eco . . . In Venetia appresso Ricciardo Amadino. 1601.* See Gaspari, vol. II, p. 229. Complete transcriptions of this and most of the other unpublished compositions mentioned in this essay are found in Kurtzman, "The Monteverdi Vespers."

32. See chapter I, pp. 19-20 and chapter III, pp. 99-102 for further commentary on *Nisi Dominus*.

33. In *Salmi Intieri che nelle Solennità dell'anno al Vespro si cantano, Con il Cantico della B. Vergine. A sei voci. Di Gio. Giacomo Gastoldi Maestro di Capella nella Chiesa Ducale di Santa Barbara di Mantoa. Con il Basso continuo per l'Organo. Libro Secondo . . . In Venetia, Appresso Ricciardo Amadino. 1607.* See Bussi, *Piacenza*, p. 48.

34. In *Sacri Fiori Mottetti à due, à tre, et à quatro voci per cantar nel organo di Leon Leoni Maestro di Capella nel Duomo di Vicenza, Con la sua partitura corrente à commodo delli organisti. Libro Primo . . . In Venetia, apresso Ricciardo Amadino. 1606.* See Gaspari, vol. II, pp. 449-450, and Sartori, *Assisi*, pp. 82-83.

35. These passages of unmeasured recitation are frequently labeled *falsibordoni* in the prints themselves, even though they may be for only one voice accompanied by organ continuo. The organist would have had to play a full chordal harmonization of the psalm tone, so the rubric *falsibordoni* in connection with a solo voice is not an inconsistency in terminology.

36. In *Il Secondo Libro de Madrigali, e Mottetti à una voce sola per cantare sopra gravicemboli, chitarroni, et organi, Con Passaggi, e senza del Molto R. P. D. Severo Bonini Monaco di Vallambrosa . . . In Firenze: Appresso Cristosano Marescotti. 1609.* See Nigel Fortune, "A Handlist of Printed Italian Secular Monody Books, 1602-1635," *R. M. A. Research Chronicle* 3 (1963): 32.

37. See chapter I, pp. 34-37 for an extensive examination of the role of instruments in the Vespers. The function of *ad libitum* instrumentation with regard to performance conditions is discussed in the Introduction, pp. 3-4.

38. *Il Primo Libro de' Concerti Ecclesiastici à 1. à 2. à 3. à 4. & à 5. Parte con voci sole, & parte con voci, & Instrumenti di Fr. Archangelo Crotti da Ferrara Agostiniano Eremita Osservante . . . In Venetia, Appresso Giacomo Vincenti. 1608.* See Gaspari, vol. II, p. 412.

39. *Motetti à dua, & tre voci, Per cantar nell'Organo con il Basso continuo, di Caterina Assandra Pavese . . . Opera Seconda . . . In Milano, Per l'herede di Simon Tini, & Filippo Lomazzo. 1609.* See Gaspari, vol. II, p. 341.

40. Modern edition by Denis Arnold, *Giovanni Gabrieli: Opera Omnia* (Rome: American Institute of Musicology, 1956—), vols. IV and V.

41. See Egon Kenton, *Life and Works of Giovanni Gabrieli*, vol. XVI of "Musicological Studies and Documents" (American Institute of Musicology, 1967), pp. 163-166, 179, and 185-188.

42. *Concerti per sonare et cantare. Di Giulio Radino Padovano Cioè Canzone, & Ricercari à Quattro, & Otto, Mottetti, Messe, Salmi, & Magnificat, à Cinque, Sei, Sette, Dieci, Dodeci, & Sedeci Voci . . . In Venetia, Appresso Angelo Gardano, & Fratelli. 1607.* See Sartori, *Bibliografia*, vol. I, p. 142 (item 1607a).

43. *Psalmi Sex, qui in Vesperis ad Concentum varietatem interponuntur, Ternis vocibus. Eosdem sequitur Completorium Quaternis vocibus. Cum Basso ad Organum. Auctore Augustino Agazario Armonico Intronato. Opus Duodecimum. Venetijs, Apud Ricciardum Amadinum. 1609.* See Edith B. Schnapper, *The British Union-Catalogue of Early Music Printed before the Year 1801* (London: Butterworths Scientific Publications, 1957), vol. I, p. 8.

44. Denis Arnold, "Giovanni Croce and the 'Concertato' Style," *Musical Quarterly* 39, no. 1 (January 1953): 44.

45. Though not precisely specified by Arnold, the collection in question is entitled *Raccolta Terza di Leonardo Simonetti Musico nella Capella della Serenissima Repubblica. De Messa et Salmi del Sig. Alessandro Grandi et Gio † Chiozotto à 2. 3. 4. con Basso continuo. Aggiontovi li Ripieni à beneplacito . . . In Venetia. 1630. Appresso Bartholomeo Magni.* See Gaspari, vol. II, pp. 83-84.

46. *Apparato Musicale di Messa, Sinfonie, Canzoni, Motetti, & Letanie della Beata Vergine. A otto voci. Con la partitura de Bassi, & un novo ordine, con che si mostra, come, & con Istromenti, & senza si possa nell'Organo rappresentare. Opera Quinta. D'Amante Franzoni Servita Academico Olimpico Maestro di Capella nella Chiesa Ducale di Santa Barbara di Mantova. Libro Primo. . . . In Venetia, Appresso Ricciardo Amadino. 1613.* See Paganelli, "Catalogo delle opere musicali," pp. 324-325.

47. See also Bonta, "The Uses of the Sonata da Chiesa," pp. 62-63. Carol Mac-Clintock notes the importance of instruments in the services at the Ducal Church of Santa Barbara during the tenure of Giaches de Wert as *maestro di cappella*. See MacClintock, *Giaches de Wert: Life and Works*, vol. XVII of "Musicological Studies and Documents" (American Institute of Musicology, 1966), pp. 148 and 154.

48. Arnold, "Monteverdi and the Technique of 'Concertato,'" p. 7.

49. Modern edition by Philippo Pedrell, *Thomae Ludovici Victoria Abulensis: Opera Omnia* (Leipzig: Breitkopf & Härtel, 1902-1911), vol. VII, pp. 1-10.

50. In *Vespertina Omnium Solemnitatum Psalmodia octonis vocibus decantanda, Auctore Ioanne A Cruce Clodiense In Ecclesia Divi Marci Musices Vice Magistro . . . Venetiis, Apud Iacobum Vincentium. 1603.* See Gaspari, vol. II, p. 213.

51. Further discussion of the role of the psalm tone in polyphonic psalm settings is found in Armstrong's as yet unpublished article, "How to Compose a Psalm."

52. An example of a psalm tone in canon is found in the *Sicut erat* of Gastoldi's

Lauda Jerusalem in *Vespertina Omnium Solemnitatum Psalmodia quinis vocibus decantanda. Io. Iacobi Gastoldi in Ecclesia Ducali Inclitae urbis Mantuae Musices Praefecti. Liber Secundus . . . Venetijs Apud Ricciardum Amadinum. 1602.* See Gaspari, vol. II, pp. 229-230.

53. An extended discussion of variation techniques in *Dixit Dominus* is found in chapter III, pp. 91-93.

54. Structural symmetry in the Vespers and *L'Orfeo* is discussed in chapter III, pp. 69-70, 86, 91-93, and 112 note 19. See also Donald J. Grout, *A Short History of Opera* (New York: Columbia University Press, 1947), pp. 60-68.

55. See examples 14a, b, and c on pp. 93-95.

56. Modern edition by Claudio Gallico, *Lodovico Viadana: Cento Concerti Ecclesiastici, Parte Prima,* vol. I of "Monumenti Musicali Mantovani" (Kassel: Bärenreiter, 1964). A *Magnificat* with a trio texture antedating Monteverdi's Vespers is found in *Musica per Cantare con L'Organo ad Una, Due, & Tre Voci, Di Tiburtio Massaino. Opera Trentesima seconda . . . In Venetia, Appresso Alessandro Raverij. 1607.* See Schnapper, *British Union-Catalogue,* vol. II, p. 660. Once again an early instance of a modern technique occurs in a *motet* collection.

57. For a more extended study of the musical organization and structure of the psalms, see chapter III, pp. 91-104 and Kurtzman, "The Monteverdi Vespers," pp. 121-170.

58. A detailed study of the relationship between the two *Magnificats* in the *Vespro* is found in chapter III, pp. 71-86.

59. The early history of polyphonic Magnificats, hymns, and psalms is treated in Masakata Kanazawa, "Polyphonic Music for Vespers during the Fifteenth Century" (Ph.D. dissertation, Harvard University, 1966). On *Cinquecento* Magnificats see Carl-Heinz Illing, *Zur Technik der Magnificat-Komposition des 16. Jahrhunderts* (Wolfenbüttel, Berlin: G. Kallmeyer, 1936).

60. Strunk, *Source Readings,* p. 270. Cerone's dependence on Ponzio in his treatment of the Magnificat is discussed in Armstrong, "How to Compose a Psalm."

61. Modern edition by Alexander Main, *Costanzo Festa: Opera Omnia* (American Institute of Musicology, 1962—), vol. II.

62. Modern editions by Higinio Anglés, *Cristóbal de Morales: Opera Omnia: XVI Magnificat,* vol. XVII of "Monumentos de la Música Española" (Barcelona: Consejo Superior de Investigaciones Científicas, 1956); and Pedrell, *Thomae Ludovici Victoria,* vol. V.

63. Modern edition by Raffaele Casimiri, *Le Opere complete di Giovanni Pierluigi da Palestrina* (Rome: Edizione Fratelli Scalera, 1939—), vol. XVI. The only book of Magnificats published by Palestrina in his lifetime did not appear until 1591.

64. See, for example, the *Magnificats* by Luigi Mazzi in *Li Salmi à cinque voci Che si cantano dalla Santa Chiesa Romana nelli Vesperi delle Solennità di tutto l'Anno, Con doi Magnificat et il Basso per l'Organo di Luigi Mazzi Organista & Maestro di Musica*

dell'Altezza Serenissima di Modena. Libro Primo . . . In Venetia Appresso Giacomo Vincenti. 1610. See Maggini, *Luca, Biblioteca del Seminario,* p. 153.

65. See chapter III, pp. 71-86.

66. In *Vespertina Omnium Solemnitatum Psalmodia . . . 1602.*

67. In *Sacri Fiori Mottetti . . . 1606.*

68. In *Musica per Cantare . . . 1607.*

69. *Passaggi sopra tutti li salmi che ordinariamente canta Santa Chiesa. Ne i Vesperi della Dominica, & ne i giorni Festivi di tutto l'anno. Con il Basso sotto per sonare, & cantare con Organo, o con altri stromenti. Fatti da Gio. Luca Conforti della Città di Mileto, Cantore nella Capella di sua santità. Libro Primo . . . In Venetia Appresso Angelo Gardano & Fratelli. 1607.* Copy at Vercelli, Archivio della Cattedrale. See *Fontes Artis Musicae,* 1958/1, p. 24.

70. *Arie Devote Le quali contengono in se la Maniera di cantar con gratia l'imitation delle parole, et altri affetti . . . In Roma appresso Simone Verovio. 1608.* See Gaspari, vol. II, p. 418.

71. See Leo Schrade, *Monteverdi: Creator of Modern Music* (New York: W. W. Norton & Company, Inc., 1950), pp. 256 and 258; Hans F. Redlich, *Claudio Monteverdi: Life and Works,* trans. Kathleen Dale (London: Oxford University Press, 1952), pp. 127-128; Denis Arnold, *Monteverdi* (London: J. M. Dent and Sons Ltd., 1963), pp. 142-143; and Guglielmo Barblan, Claudio Gallico, and Guido Pannain, *Claudio Monteverdi* (Turin: Edizioni RAI Radiotelevisione italiana, 1967), p. 337. Arnold discusses a few related pieces by other composers in "Notes on two Movements of the Monteverdi 'Vespers'" and "Monteverdi's Church Music: some Venetian Traits."

72. Structural aspects of the *Sonata* are discussed in chapter III, pp. 86-91.

73. Arnold, "Notes," pp. 60-63.

74. See note 46 above.

75. Edward E. Lowinsky, *Secret Chromatic Art in the Netherlands Motet* (New York: Russell & Russell, 1946), pp. 16-26. A recent dissertation on this subject, which I have not yet seen, is by Mary E. Columbro, "Ostinato Technique in the Franco-Flemish motet: 1480-ca. 1562" (Case Western Reserve University, 1974).

76. Arnold, "Monteverdi's Church Music," pp. 84-86.

77. Ibid.

78. In *Motecta Octonis Vocibus Antonii Gualterii in terra D. Danielis Musices Magistri, Liber Primus. Venetiis, Apud Iacobum Vincentium. 1604.* This composition was kindly called to my attention by Don Siro Cisilino of the Cini Foundation in Venice.

79. Christiane Engelbrecht, "Eine Sonata con voce von Giovanni Gabrieli," *Bericht über den internationalen musikwissenschaftlichen Kongress Hamburg 1956* (Kassel:

Bärenreiter Verlag, 1957), pp. 88-89. This piece is as yet unpublished.

80. *Ignatii Donati Ecclesiae Metropolitanae Urbini Musicae Praefecti. Sacri Concentus Unis, Binis, Ternis, Quaternis, & Quinis vocibus, Una cum parte Organica . . . Venetiis, Apud Iacobum Vincentium. 1612.* See Gaspari, vol. II, p. 414 and Bohn, *Bibliographie der Musik-Druckwerke*, p. 114.

81. Part of Donati's preface, describing the manner of performance, is translated in Arnold, "Monteverdi's Church Music," p. 87.

82. See, for example, Redlich, *Claudio Monteverdi*, p. 127; Schrade, *Monteverdi*, p. 262; and Arnold, *Monteverdi*, p. 141.

83. Modern edition by Michel Sanvoisin, *Giovanni Gabrieli: Canzoni e Sonate*, vol. XXVII of "Le Pupitre" (Paris: Heugel & Cie., 1971).

84. For a complete list of the publications in which these settings are found, see Kurtzman, "The Monteverdi Vespers," Appendix D. Several additional settings, including some by German composers, are found in the second part of Johannes Donfrid's *Promptuarum Musicum* published in 1623. See RISM 6123[2]. See also chapter III, pp. 108-110. The text is derived from Isaiah 6:2-3 and the First Epistle of John 5:7.

85. Pedrell, *Thomae Ludovici Victoria*, vol. I, pp. 36-39.

86. In *Liber Sacrarum Cantionum quae ad septem, octo, novem, decem, duodecim, sexdecim voces choris . . . 1589.* See Bussi, *Piacenza*, p. 59.

87. In *Ioannis Francisci Anerii Sacerdotis Romani, Musicorum in Ecclesia Deiparae Virginis ad Montes Concentuum Compositoris. Singulis, binis, ternisque vocibus. Liber Primus. Cum Basso ad Organum. Romae, Apud Io. Baptistam Roblettum. 1609.* See Sartori, *Assisi*, p. 20.

88. See the translations of the foreword to Caccini's *Le Nuove Musiche* of 1602 in Strunk, *Source Readings*, pp. 384-389, and in H. Wiley Hitchcock, ed., *Giulio Caccini: Le Nuove Musiche* (Madison: A-R Editions, Inc., 1970), pp. 43-56.

89. *Gio. Francisci Capello Veneti Fesulanae Congregationis Filij Sacrorum Concentuum Unica, & Duabus Vocibus cum Litanijs B. Virginis Mariae. Opus Primum. Venetijs, apud Ricciardum Amadinum, 1610.* See Gaspari, vol. II, pp. 390-391. This collection and other music by Capello is discussed in my article "Giovanni Francesco Capello, an Avant-Gardist of the Early Seventeenth Century," *Musica Disciplina* 31 (1977): 155-182.

90. In *Giardino di Spirituali Concenti A Due, A Tre, e A Quattro Voci, Con il Basso per l'Organo. Di Hercole Porta Organista della Colleggiata di S. Giovanni Impersicetto . . . In Venetia, Appresso Alessandro Raverij. 1609.* See Bohn, *Bibliographie der Musik-Druckwerke bis 1700*, p. 312.

91. For a list of publications in which settings of these texts are found, see Kurtzman, "The Monteverdi Vespers," Appendices E and F.

92. Durante, *Arie Devote . . . 1608* and Bonini, *Il Secondo Libro de Madrigali, e Mottetti . . . 1609.*

93. Capello, *Sacrorum Concentuum . . . 1610.* Alessandro Grandi, *Il Primo Libro de Motteti à due, tre, quatro, cinque, & otto voci, con una Messa à quatro. Accommodati per cantarsi nell'Organo, Clavicembalo, Chitarone, o altro simile Stromento. Con il Basso per sonare di Alessandro Grandi Maestro di Capella del Spirito Santo in Ferrara . . . In Venetia, Appresso Giacomo Vincenti, 1610.* See Gaspari, vol. II, pp. 390-391 and 430. For a discussion of the relationship between these two collections and the Monteverdi Vespers, see Kurtzman, "The Monteverdi Vespers," pp. 383-387. See also note 89 above.

94. See above, pp. 124-127.

95. *Liber Primus Concentus, in Duos Distincti Choros, In quibus Vespere Missa, sacraeque Cantiones in Nativitate, Beatae Mariae Virginis aliarumque Virginam Festivitatibus decantandi continentur. Authore, R. Don Io. Petro Flaccomio Siculo, e Civitate Milatis. Venetiis, Apud Angelum Gardanum, & Fratres. 1611.* See Rafael Mitjana, *Catalogue critique et descriptif des imprimés de musique des XVIe et XVIIe siècles, conservés à la Bibliothèque de l'Université Royale d'Upsala,* 3 vols. (Uppsala: Impr. Almqvist & Wiksell, 1911-1951), columns 112-113. Flaccomio's is another of the collections devoted specifically to Marian Vespers.

96. *Concerti Ecclesiastici alla moderna dove si contengono Messa, Salmi per il Vespero, e Compieta, & Magnificat à Tre, à Quattro, à Cinque, à Sei, à Sette, & à Otto di D. Grisostomo Rubiconi da Rimini Monaco Olivetano Organista di S. Benedetto Novello in Padua Con il Basso continuo per Sonare nell'Organo. Opera Seconda . . . In Venetia, Appresso Giacomo Vincenti. 1611.* See Gaspari, vol. II, p. 135; Schnapper, *British Union-Catalogue,* vol. II, p. 906; and Paganelli, "Catalogo delle opere musicali," p. 335.

97. Monteverdi's *Magnificat à 4 in genere da Capella,* published in the *Selva Morale e Spirituale* of 1640 (1641), employs the Magnificat tone as a *cantus firmus* in several verses, but without its assuming the structural significance witnessed in the 1610 Vespers. This later *Magnificat* is in the *stile antico* and resembles the Marian canticles of Victoria.

98. *Lamentationi Benedictus, e Miserere da cantarsi il Mercordì, Giovedì, e Venerdì Santo di sera à Matutino. Concertate à Cinque Voci, et Istromenti à beneplacito. Dal R. P. Gio. Francesco Capello da Venetia, della Congregat. Fiesolana. Opera Terza . . . In Verona, Appresso Angelo Tamo. 1612.* Attention was first called to Capello's *Lamentationi* by Denis Arnold in "Giovanni Croce and the 'Concertato' Style," p. 42.

99. See notes 89 and 93.

100. *Sacrorum Concentuum . . . 1610.*

101. *Salmi Intieri che si cantano al Vespro In alcune Solennità de l'Anno con due Magnificat. Il tutto concertato à Quattro Voci co'l Basso continuo per l'Organo. Aggiuntevi ancora le parti per due Istrumenti Gravi, & Acuto per chi hà tal commodità. Opera Quinta. Di D. Antonio Burlini da Rovigo Monaco Olivetano . . . In Venetia, Appresso Giacomo Vincenti. 1613.* See Giuseppe Turrini, *Il patrimonio musicale della Biblioteca Capitolare di Verona dal sec. XV al XIX* (Verona: La Tipografica Veronese, 1952), p. 41. *Messa Salmi, et Motetti Concertati à Otto Voci in due Chori col Basso*

continuo per l'Organo, & una parte per un Violino per chi n'hà commodità. Opera Ottava.
Di D. Antonio Burlini Monaco Olivetano . . . In Venetia, Appresso Giacomo Vincenti.
1615. See Gaspari, vol. II, p. 46.

102. Burlini's *Riviera Fiorita di Concerti Musicale,* published in Venice in 1612, names
him as *"Organista di Santa Elena di Venetia."* However, his *Fiori di Concerti Spirituali,*
also published in Venice in 1612, indicates that he is now *"Organista di Monteoliveto*
Maggiore di Siena." See Gaspari, vol. II, p. 388.

103. In *Sacrorum Canticorum una, duabus, tribus, quatuor, et quinque vocibus, D.*
Seraphini Pattae Mediolanensis Monachi Cassinensis, & in Ecclesia Sancti Salvatoris Papiae
Organistae Liber Secundus cui inseruntur Cantiones quaedam instrumentis tantum ac-
commodatae, cum parte infima pro Organo . . . Venetijs Apud Iacobum Vincentium. 1613.
See Gaspari, vol. II, p. 477 and Sartori, *Bibliografia,* vol. II, pp. 58-59.

104. *Messa, e Salmi da Concertarsi nel'Organo et anco con diversi Stromenti, à*
Cinque Voci, & insieme Sinfonie, & Motetti à Una, Due, Tre, Quattro, Cinque & Sei Voci
di Francesco Usper Organista nella Chiesa di S. Salvatore di Venetia . . . In Venetia,
Appresso Giacomo Vincenti. 1614. See Gaspari, vol. II, p. 147. Usper's psalms constitute
the "male *cursus.*"

105. *Messa Vespro et Compieta à cinque voci col suo basso continuo Aggiuntovi un*
Violino, & Corneto per le Sinfonie, & per li Ripieni. Di Amadio Freddi Maestro di Capella
nel Duomo di Treviso . . . In Venetia, 1616. Appresso Ricciardo Amadino. See Gaspari,
vol. II, p. 72. Freddi's is another of the collections containing the five psalms for Vespers
of the Virgin.

106. *Psalmi Magnif. cum quatuor antiphonis ad Vesperas Octo Vocib. Una cum Basso*
ad Organum Decantandi Auctore Paulo Tardito Romano in Ecclesia SS. Iacobi, & Illefonsi
Hispanicae Nationis, Musices Moderatore. Liber Secundus. Romae. Apud Luca Antonium
Soldum 1620. See Bussi, *Piacenza,* p. 97. Tardito's five psalms in the conservative style
form the "male *cursus.*"

107. See Armstrong, "The Vesper Psalms," and Anne Schnoebelen, "Cazzati vs.
Bologna: 1657-1671," *Musical Quarterly* **57,** no. 1 (January 1971): 26-39. Catalogues of
Italian and other European libraries reveal the enormous quantity of music for Vespers that
poured from Cazzati's pen. The survival of these collections in many locales suggests that
their use was widespread in the seventeenth century.